CAMBRIDGE LIBRARY COLLECTION

Books of enduring scholarly value

Religion

For centuries, scripture and theology were the focus of prodigious amounts of scholarship and publishing, dominated in the English-speaking world by the work of Protestant Christians. Enlightenment philosophy and science, anthropology, ethnology and the colonial experience all brought new perspectives, lively debates and heated controversies to the study of religion and its role in the world, many of which continue to this day. This series explores the editing and interpretation of religious texts, the history of religious ideas and institutions, and not least the encounter between religion and science.

The Didascalia Apostolorum in English

The twin sisters Agnes Lewis (1843–1926) and Margaret Gibson (1843–1920) were pioneering biblical scholars who became experts in a number of ancient languages. Travelling widely in the Middle East, they made several significant discoveries, including one of the earliest manuscripts of the four gospels in Syriac, the language believed to have been spoken by Jesus himself. Previously published in the Horae Semitica series, this second fascicule contains Gibson's English translation of the the Didascalia Apostolorum. Traditionally attributed to the apostles, the text is a treatise on Church law and doctrine, and the volume includes additional material supplied by Gibson from a variety of sources. Covering topics including church organisation, charity and forgiveness, Gibson described the Didascalia as a 'potent instrument' used to gain the 'unquestioning obedience of the Christian people.' An early precursor to the Apostolic Constitutions, this text is of considerable significance to ecclesiastical history.

Cambridge University Press has long been a pioneer in the reissuing of out-of-print titles from its own backlist, producing digital reprints of books that are still sought after by scholars and students but could not be reprinted economically using traditional technology. The Cambridge Library Collection extends this activity to a wider range of books which are still of importance to researchers and professionals, either for the source material they contain, or as landmarks in the history of their academic discipline.

Drawing from the world-renowned collections in the Cambridge University Library, and guided by the advice of experts in each subject area, Cambridge University Press is using state-of-the-art scanning machines in its own Printing House to capture the content of each book selected for inclusion. The files are processed to give a consistently clear, crisp image, and the books finished to the high quality standard for which the Press is recognised around the world. The latest print-on-demand technology ensures that the books will remain available indefinitely, and that orders for single or multiple copies can quickly be supplied.

The Cambridge Library Collection will bring back to life books of enduring scholarly value (including out-of-copyright works originally issued by other publishers) across a wide range of disciplines in the humanities and social sciences and in science and technology.

The Didascalia Apostolorum in English

Edited and Translated by
Margaret Dunlop Gibson

CAMBRIDGE UNIVERSITY PRESS

Cambridge, New York, Melbourne, Madrid, Cape Town,
Singapore, São Paolo, Delhi, Tokyo, Mexico City

Published in the United States of America by Cambridge University Press, New York

www.cambridge.org
Information on this title: www.cambridge.org/9781108018975

This edition first published 1903
This digitally printed version 2011

ISBN 978-1-108-01897-5 Paperback

THE DIDASCALIA APOSTOLORUM IN ENGLISH

London: C. J. CLAY AND SONS,
CAMBRIDGE UNIVERSITY PRESS WAREHOUSE,
AVE MARIA LANE.
Glasgow: 50, WELLINGTON STREET.

Leipzig: F. A. BROCKHAUS.
New York: THE MACMILLAN COMPANY.
Bombay and Calcutta: MACMILLAN AND CO., LTD.

HORAE SEMITICAE No. II

THE
DIDASCALIA APOSTOLORUM
IN ENGLISH

TRANSLATED FROM THE SYRIAC

BY

MARGARET DUNLOP GIBSON M.R.A.S.
LL.D. (St Andrews)

LONDON
C. J. CLAY AND SONS
CAMBRIDGE UNIVERSITY PRESS WAREHOUSE
AVE MARIA LANE
1903

Cambridge:
PRINTED BY J. AND C. F. CLAY,
AT THE UNIVERSITY PRESS.

INTRODUCTION.

IN preparing an English translation of the *Didascalia Apostolorum* from the Syriac (the original Greek being lost), I have been guided by the consideration that the student of Ecclesiastical History ought to familiarize himself with the ideas and practices of bygone ages, and that it is especially useful to us to know by what means the clergy, in the early centuries of our era, obtained for themselves, whether for good or evil, the unquestioning obedience of Christian people. To this end, the *Didascalia Apostolorum* must have been a potent instrument. As passages of it are quoted by St Epiphanius, who lived in the fourth century, we cannot doubt that it is of early date; but whatever the precise period at which it was first promulgated, it evidently came forth clothed with the supposed authority of our Lord's Apostles. When we have got over our initial amazement that any body of ecclesiastical rulers should attempt to use the names of their predecessors instead of their own, we must acknowledge that most of the precepts and practices inculcated are excellent, and well worthy of our own consideration; such as the directions to Bishops as to how they are to use the gifts brought to the Church for their own support and for the relief of the poor (Ch. VIII.), and those for the reception of strangers during Divine service (Ch. XII.). To some minds, no doubt, this document, from its early date, will appeal with greater force than to others; and to these I would respectfully suggest that if they consider it to be really of Apostolic authority, they ought to adopt its rules in their entirety; but that it is not legitimate to accept one and reject another, unless that other be proved to be a later interpolation. For instance, if implicit obedience is to be given to Bishops (Ch. IX. p. 48), they, the Bishops, must be elected by all the people[1] (Ch. III. p. 10). Some of the rules are now, through the progress of civilization, rendered unnecessary and obsolete.

[1] Mrs Lewis found this custom existing in Cyprus, and was told that it prevails also in many parts of Greece.

I have endeavoured to translate each Syriac word by an English word conveying its original meaning, and to avoid any expression that savours of ambiguity. I am glad to see that Professor Nau also translates ܟܗܢܐ = *ἱερεὺς*, alone as "priest," and ܩܫܝܫܐ = *πρεσβύτερος*, which I call "Elder," he calls "vieillard." He has not condescended to adopt the still more appropriate word "ancien," used by his Protestant countrymen; and is obliged, in consequence, still further to explain it by drawing attention to the fact that the persons in question are not laymen (*La Didascalie*, Paris, 1902, note, p. 75).

The most salient feature of the *Didascalia* is its exaltation of the authority of the Bishops; yet it is noteworthy that there is no mention of the Bishops of Rome as superior over other Bishops. So far does the author go in the claim he makes for them, that M. Nau is impelled to introduce a foot-note to the passage at the foot of p. 51, to the effect that "it looks as if the author of the *Didascalia* had been a Bishop." Whether this were so or not, he had evidently forgotten our Lord's injunction to the Apostles: "It shall not be so among you." It is curious how the writers of this apocryphal literature loved to take Clement of Rome as their imagined author.

The quotations from the *Didascalia* in the writings of Epiphanius are given by Lagarde in Bunsen's *Christianity and Mankind*, Vol. III. pp. 41, 42. They are as follows (from Migne, as the Basle edition of 1544 is not in the University Library, and Lagarde's citations from it contain several misprints).

Epiph. adv. haereses, *κατὰ Σευηριανῶν*, p. 170, ed. Basiliensis 1544: Migne (Paris 1858) I. 836. *Ἀλλὰ καὶ οἱ ἀπόστολοί φασιν ἐν τῇ Διατάξει τῇ καλουμένῃ, ὅτι φυτεία Θεοῦ καὶ ἀμπελὼν ἡ καθολικὴ ἐκκλησία.*

Against the Severians. And the Apostles say in the so-called Constitution, that the planting and vineyard of God is the Catholic Church. See p. 2, ll. 9, 10.

κατὰ Αὐδιανῶν, p. 350, Basil.: Migne II. 356, 357. *Οἱ αὐτοὶ Αὐδιανοὶ παραφέρουσι τὴν τῶν ἀποστόλων Διάταξιν .... περὶ τοῦ πάσχα .... ὁρίζουσι γὰρ ἐν τῇ αὐτῇ Διατάξει οἱ ἀπόστολοι ὅτι ὑμεῖς μὴ ψηφίζητε, ἀλλὰ ποιεῖτε ὅταν οἱ ἀδελφοὶ ὑμῶν οἱ ἐκ περιτομῆς. Μετ' αὐτῶν ἅμα ποιεῖτε· καὶ οὐκ εἶπαν, Ὅταν οἱ ἀδελφοὶ ὑμῶν οἱ ἐν περιτομῇ, ἀλλά, οἱ ἐκ περιτομῆς, ἵνα δείξωσι τοὺς ἀπὸ τῆς περιτομῆς εἰς τὴν Ἐκκλησίαν μετελθόντας ἀρχηγοὺς εἶναι μετ' ἐκεῖνον τὸν χρόνον .... Παρὰ τοῖς ἀποστόλοις δὲ τὸ ῥητὸν δι' ὁμόνοιαν ἐμφέρεται, ὡς ἐπιμαρτυροῦσι λέγοντες, ὅτι, Κἄν τε πλανηθῶσι μηδὲ ὑμῖν μελέτω .... φάσκουσι γὰρ τὴν ἀγρυπνίαν φέρειν, μεσαζόντων τῶν ἀζύμων.*

Against the Audaeans. The same Audaeans mention the Constitution of the Apostles .... about the Passover .... for the Apostles define in that Constitution that ye reckon not, but observe [it] when your brethren from the circumcision do; do so together with them; and they did not say, "when your brethren in the circumcision," but "those from the circumcision," that they might show that those who had come over into the church from the circumcision were leaders after that time; with Apostles this is enjoined for the sake of harmony, as they testify, saying that even if they err it is no matter to you .... they say to keep vigil in the midst of the feast of unleavened bread. See p. 97, l. 33.

Ibid. p. 351: Migne II. 360, 361. *Λέγουσι γὰρ οἱ αὐτοὶ ἀπόστολοι, ὅτι, Ὅταν ἐκεῖνοι εὐωχῶνται, ὑμεῖς νηστεύοντες ὑπὲρ αὐτῶν πενθεῖτε, ὅτι ἐν τῇ ἡμέρᾳ τῆς ἑορτῆς τὸν Χριστὸν ἐσταύρωσαν. Καὶ ὅταν αὐτοὶ πενθῶσι τὰ ἄζυμα ἐσθίοντες ἐν πικρῖσιν, ὑμεῖς εὐωχεῖσθε.*

The same Apostles say that when they (*i.e.* the Jews) feast, do ye mourn over them with fasting, because in the day of the feast they crucified the Christ; and when they are mourning, eating unleavened bread with bitter herbs, do ye feast. See p. 99, l. 29.

Et mox: Migne II. 361. *Αὐτῶν ἀκούοντες ἐν τῇ Διατάξει, ὅτι Ὁ κακῶν ἑαυτοῦ τὴν ψυχὴν ἐν Κυριακῇ, ἐπικατάρατός ἐστι τῷ Θεῷ.*

Hearing them in the Constitution, that he who vexeth his soul on Sunday is accursed with God. See p. 100, last line.

Ibid.: Migne II. 364. *Παρατηρεῖται δὲ ἡ Ἐκκλησία ἄγειν τὴν ἑορτὴν τοῦ Πάσχα, τουτέστι τὴν ἑβδομάδα τὴν ὡρισμένην, καὶ ἀπ' αὐτῶν τῶν ἀποστόλων ἐν τῇ Διατάξει, ἀπὸ δευτέρας σαββάτων, ὅπερ ἐστὶν ἀγορασμὸς τοῦ προβάτου.*

The Church takes care to keep the feast of the Passover, that is to say, the appointed week, and from the Apostles themselves in the Constitution from the second [day] of the week, when the purchase of the lamb takes place. See p. 98, l. 24.

κατὰ Ἀερίου, p. 387, Basil.: Migne II. 512, 513. *Εἰ δὲ καὶ χρὴ τὸ τῆς Διατάξεως τῶν ἀποστόλων λέγειν, πῶς ἐκεῖ ὡρίζοντο τετράδα καὶ προσάββατον νηστείαν διὰ παντὸς χωρὶς Πεντηκοστῆς; καὶ περὶ τῶν ἓξ ἡμερῶν τοῦ Πάσχα πῶς παραγγέλλουσι μηδὲν ὅλως λαμβάνειν ἢ ἄρτου καὶ ἁλὸς καὶ ὕδατος; Ποίαν τε ἡμέραν ἄγειν, πῶς τε ἀπολύειν εἰς ἐπιφώσκουσαν Κυριακὴν, φανερόν ἐστι.... Εἶτα δὲ εἰ μὴ περὶ τῆς αὐτῆς ὑποθέσεως Τετράδων καὶ Προσαββάτων οἱ αὐτοὶ ἀπόστολοι ἐν τῇ Διατάξει ἔλεγον, καὶ ἄλλως ἐκ πανταχόθεν εἴχομεν ἀποδεῖξαι, ὅμως περὶ τούτου ἀκριβῶς γράφουσι.*

Against Aerius. Is it necessary to quote that of the Constitution of the Apostles how there they appointed Thursday and Friday as a fast continually except during Pentecost; and about the six days of the Passover, how they recommend to partake of nothing whatever but bread and salt and water? what kind of day to keep, and how to release as Sunday dawns, is evident .... afterwards if not about the same subject of Thursdays and Fridays the same Apostles said in the Constitution, we could even show otherwise from all quarters how they write accurately about this. See pp. 98, 99.

κατὰ Μασσαλιανῶν, p. 452, Basil.: Migne II. 765, 768. *Καὶ περὶ μὲν οὖν τοῦ γενείου ἐν ταῖς Διατάξεσι τῶν ἀποστόλων φάσκει ὁ θεῖος λόγος καὶ ἡ διδασκαλία μὴ φθείρειν, τουτέστι μὴ τέμνειν τρίχας γενείου, μηδὲ ἑταιρισμῷ κατακομεῖσθαι* (or *κατακοσμεῖσθαι*), *μήτε ὑπερηφανίας ὑπόδειγμα δικαιοσύνης τὴν προσέλευσιν ἔχειν.*

Against the Massalians. About the beard in the Constitutions of the Apostles, the Divine word and the *Didascalia* say, not to destroy it, that is to say, not to cut the hairs of the beard, nor to adorn oneself for harlotry, nor have the approach of righteousness as a sign of arrogance. See p. 4, ll. 33–35.

I have in this translation incorporated or indicated the variants of Codex Sangerman and others only when they present anything of value. The Syriac student will find all the variants given in the preceding volume, and to the English reader most of them would be of little, or no interest. I have brought my translation to a close at the end of Chapter XXVI., which Professor Nau considers to be its natural termination (*La Didascalie*, p. 166).

Perhaps the most valuable part of the text is the multitude of Scriptural quotations included in it. As I have said in the Introduction to the previous volume, those from the Old Testament are all from the Septuagint, and I subjoin a list of them. Those from the New Testament are, as was to be expected, mostly from the Peshitta, the authorized version of the Syrian Church, which has held its own, with hardly any variants, for about fifteen centuries. It is therefore remarkable to find some quotations which in their choice of expressions coincide preferably with the Old Syriac, and this is more than we should have expected, considering how many times the *Didascalia* must have been copied, and how strong the tendency would be for each succeeding scribe to supply the quotation from the version with which he was familiar. There are also a large number of New Testament quotations which coincide neither with the

Old Syriac nor with the Peshitta. The most probable explanation is the conjecture of Lagarde with regard to the Apostolic Constitutions[1], which are an amplification of the *Didascalia*, viz. that the immediate source from which the author drew was a Gospel Harmony. Professor Nau says of the *Didascalia* "elle parait ignorer l'Evangile de S. Jean" (*La Didascalie*, footnote, p. 119). Nevertheless it will be seen from our list of quotations that there are several which can only be taken from the Fourth Gospel. I have endeavoured to classify all the quotations according to the best of my judgment as follows, on p. xiii.

[1] See Lagarde, *Const. Apost.* p. vii (London, 1862).

CONTENTS.

QUOTATIONS FROM THE OLD TESTAMENT CONTAINED IN THE DIDASCALIA.

PSALMS.

PROVERBS.

ISAIAH.

JEREMIAH.

JEREMIAH *cont.*

EZEKIEL.

DANIEL.

HOSEA.

JOEL.

HABAKKUK.

ZECHARIAH.

MALACHI.

TOBIT.

PRAYER OF MANASSEH

LIST OF QUOTATIONS FROM THE NEW TESTAMENT CONTAINED IN THE DIDASCALIA, CLASSIFIED.

(C. *signifies Cureton*, L. *Lewis.*)

Peshitta.

MATTHEW.

v. 11 *almost*	f. 17 a
v. 17	72 b
v. 44 *almost*	54 b
vi. 21	51 a
vii. 2[1]	39 b
vii. 2[1]	42 b
vii. 16 (L. *lost*)	71 a
x. 5[2] (C. *lost*)	71 b
x. 13 (C. *lost*)	54 b
x. 24[2] (C. *lost*)	74 a
x. 28[1] (C. *lost*)	59 b
xi. 15	17 a
xxiii. 19 *almost*	74 b
xxiii. 38 *almost* (C. *lost*) ...	67 b
xxv. 35[2] (O. S. *lost*)	59 a
xxv. 36[1] (C. *lost*)	59 a
xxv. 36[3] (C. *lost*)	59 a
xxv. 38[2] (C. *lost*)	59 a
xxvii. 25 (C. *lost*)	64 a

MARK.

ii. 17 (C. *lost*) ...	f. 23 a, 38 b
ii. 19 *almost* (O. S. *lost*) ...	63 a

LUKE.

vi. 40[1] (C. *lost*)	f. 60 b
vi. 46 (C. *lost*)	75 b
x. 16 *almost*	27 b, 34 a
xxi. 18, 19	60 b

ACTS.

viii. 20	f. 68 a
x. 9–16	70 a
xv. 8–11	70 a

ROMANS.

iii. 15–17	f. 23 b

GALATIANS.

iii. 13	f. 73 b

EPHESIANS.

iv. 26	f. 43 a

II. THESSALONIANS.

iii. 10	f. 48 b

Old Syriac.

MATTHEW.

vi. 11 (C.) ... ... f. 59 b
v. 12 ... ... 17 a
v. 18 (L. *quite*, C. *almost*) ... 72 b
v. 20 ... ... 36 a
v. 23 ... ... 43 a
vi. 10 (L. *lost*) ... ... 44 a
x. 5[1] (C. *lost*) ... ... 48 a
x. 37 *almost* ... ... 59 b
xi. 28 (C.) ... 5 a, 35 b, 70 b, 73 b
xii. 43 ... ... 74 b
xii. 44 *almost* ... ... 75 a
xviii. 10 (C.) ... ... 22 a
xviii. 17[2] (C.) ... ... 37 b
xviii. 18[1] ... . f. 17 b
xix. 4 *almost* ... ... 69 b
xxvi. 22 *almost* (C. *lost*) ... 63 a
xxvi. 23 (C. *lost*) ... ... 63 a

MARK.

xii. 42 *almost* (C. *lost*) ... f. 52 a

LUKE.

vi. 37[2] (C. *lost*) ... ... f. 39 b

JOHN.

xiii. 5 *almost* (C. *lost*) ... f. 55 b *note*

Old Syriac and Peshiṭta.

MATTHEW.

v. 5, 7 ... ... f. 14 b
v. 8 *almost* ... ... 15 a
v. 9 ... ... 15 a, 42 a
v. 22[1] ... ... 43 a
v. 24 *almost* ... ... 43 a
vi. 3 ... ... 41 b, 53 b
vi. 12 (L. *lost*) ... ... 24 a
vii. 1 (L. *lost*) ... ... 36 b
vii. 3 (L. *lost*) ... ... 21 b
vii. 5 (L. *lost*) ... ... 21 b
vii. 6 *almost* (L. *lost*) ... 50 a
vii. 15 *almost* ... ... 71 a
viii. 12[2] *almost* ... ... 60 a *note*
ix. 2 last clause (C. *lost*) ... 23 a
x. 24[1] (C. *lost*) ... ... 74 a
x. 32 *almost* ... ... 59 a
x. 33 *almost* ... ... 59 b, 60 a *note*
xi. 29, 30 *almost* ... 35 b, 70 b
xii. 30 *almost* (L. *lost*) 44 a, 46 b
xii. 31, 32 *almost* ... ... 71 b
xii. 32 ... ... 71 b
xii. 36 *almost* ... ... 14 b
xii. 45 *almost* ... ... 75 a
xiii. 16 ... ... 73 b *note*
xvi. 6 *almost* ... ... 71 b
xviii. 16[2] ... ... 37 b
xviii. 18 ... ... 22 a
xviii. 21 *almost* ... ... 42 a
xviii. 21, 22 *almost* ... ... 42 a
xix. 5, 6 *almost* ... ... f. 69 b
xix. 19 (C.) ... ... 37 a
xx. 16 ... ... 74 a *note*
xxi. 13 (L. *lost*) ... ... 21 b
xxi. 46[2] *almost* ... ... 63 a
xxii. 32 ... ... 75 a *note*
xxiii. 20, 21, 22 *almost* ... 74 b „
xxiv. 12, 13 (C. *lost*) ... 71 a
xxv. 35[3] (C. *lost*) ... ... 59 a
xxv. 39[2] (C. *lost*) ... ... 59 a
xxv. 46[2] (C. *lost*) ... ... 59 a
xxvi. 15[2] (C. *lost*) ... ... 63 b
xxvi. 21[2] *almost* (C. *lost*) ... 63 a
xxvi. 41[1] *almost* (C. *lost*) ... 60 a

MARK.

vii. 6 *almost* (C. *lost*) ... f. 36 b
viii. 37 *almost* (C. *lost*) ... 59 b
x. 21 (C. *lost*) ... ... 36 a
xii. 26 (C. *lost*) ... ... 75 a *note*
xx. 25 ... ... 41 b

LUKE.

vi. 46 (C. *lost*) ... ... f. 76 a
x. 5 *almost* ... ... 54 b
x. 7[2] (L.) ... ... 10 b
xi. 23 *almost* ... ... 44 a
xvi. 15[2] *almost* (C. *lost*) ... 13 a

JOHN.

xiii. 4[2] (C. *lost*) ... ... f. 55 b *note*

Neither.

* This has been printed by mistake on p. ܡܐ as Matt. xviii. 12.

DIDASCALIA.

TRANSLATION.

"IN the name of the Father Almighty, and of the Eternal Word and only Son, and of the Holy Ghost, one true God. We begin to write the Book *Didascalia*, as the holy Apostles of our Lord appointed to us, with regard to the presiding officers of the Holy Church, and the Canons and the Laws for believers as they commanded in it. f. 1 b

We, then, twelve Apostles of the only Son, the Everlasting Word of God, our Lord and God and Saviour Jesus the Christ, being assembled with one accord in Jerusalem the city of the great King, and with us our brother Paul, the Apostle of the Gentiles, and James the Bishop of the above-mentioned city, have established this Didascalia, in which are included the Confession and the Creed, and we have named all the Ordinances, as the ordinances of the heavenly bodies, and thus again the Ordinances of the Holy Church. We assert that every one shall stand and confess and believe in what has been allotted to him by God; that is to say, the Bishop as a shepherd; the Elders as teachers; the Deacons as ministers; the Subdeacons as helpers; the Lectors as readers; the Singers as psalmists with intelligence and with constancy; and that the rest of the populace should be hearers of the words of the Gospel according to discipline. When we had completed and confirmed these Canons, we established them in the Church. And now we have written this other Book of doctrine which will enlighten all the habitable earth, and we have sent it by the hands of Clement our comrade. This which ye hear, O Christian Nazarenes, who are beneath the sun [is] that ye may learn with diligence and care. He who hears and keeps these commandments which are written in this Didascalia, will have everlasting life, and great boldness before the judgment-seat of our Lord Jesus the Christ the Son of God, He who taught us about His great mystery. And he who is contentious, and doth not keep them, they shall put him out as an opposer and quarreller, as it is written that those who do evil things shall go to f. 2 a everlasting torment, and those who do good things shall inherit everlasting life in the kingdom of heaven.

In it there are twenty-seven chapters.

CHAPTER I.

Teaches all men in general about the simple and natural law, that what is hateful to thyself thou shouldest not do to thy neighbour * * * *"

(Codex Sangerman *cf.* Lagarde.

"The Didascalia, or the Catholic Teaching of the Twelve Apostles and holy Disciples of our Saviour.

Apostolical Constitutions Book I. Chapter I. [*About the simple and natural law.*] The planting of God, and the holy Vine of His Catholic Church, the chosen people who trust in the simplicity of the fear of the Lord, those who by their faith inherit the eternal kingdom, those who have received the power and communion of the Holy Ghost, with which they are armed and confirmed in His worship, those who have been partakers in the sprinkling of the pure and precious blood of the great God, Jesus the Christ; those who have received boldness to call God the Almighty 'Father,' as heirs and partakers with His Son [and] His Beloved; hear the Teaching of God, ye who hope for and expect His promises, according as it was written by order of our Saviour, and is in accordance with His glorious commandments! Take care, ye sons of God, and do everything so as to obey God, and in all things be pleasing to the Lord our God. If any man run after iniquity, and oppose the will of God, he shall be counted by God as an heathen and an evildoer. Flee therefore and get far from all")

Ap. Con. Bk. I. ch. i. f. 3 a Exodus xx. 17 avarice and iniquity, that ye may covet nothing from any one, for it is written in the Law, "Thou shalt not covet anything from thy neighbour, neither his field nor his house nor his servant nor his maidservant nor his ox nor his ass nor any of his goods, for all these desires are of the Evil One. For he that coveteth his neighbour's wife or his servant or his maidservant is already a thief and an adulterer." He is guilty of abomination, like a Sodomite, from our Lord and Teacher Jesus the Christ, to whom be glory and honour for ever and ever, Amen. As also in the Gospel He reneweth and confirmeth and completeth the Ten Commandments of the Law. For it is written in the Law, Thou shalt not commit adultery. But this I say unto you, as He who spoke in the Law of Moses, thus in **Matt. v. 28** person I myself say unto you, that every one who looketh at the wife of his friend to lust after her, hath already committed adultery with her in his heart. Thus he that lusteth is guilty as an adulterer. Also he that coveteth the ox or the ass of his neighbour is likely to steal it and to lead it away. Again, he that coveteth the field of his neighbour, behold, doth he not wish to narrow it at the border, and to contrive

to buy it to himself for nothing? Wherefore because of this, murders and deaths and condemnations come upon them from God. But to those men who are obedient to God there is one simple and valid law, and I say that thou shalt not make questions to Christians, this, that whatever thou hatest should happen to thyself from another, thou shalt not do to another. Thou dost not wish that any one should look at thy wife in an evil manner, for her corruption? do not thou also look at the wife of thy neighbour with an evil mind. Thou dost not wish that any one should take from thee thy garment? do not thou also take the garment of others. Thou dost not wish to be cursed or beaten? also do not thou do either
of these things to others; but if any one curseth thee, thou shalt surely **Ap. Con. I. ii.**
bless him, for it is written in the book of [1]the Psalms[1], "He that blesseth **Numbers xxiv. 9** *sic*
shall be blessed, and he that curseth shall be cursed," and again also f. 3 b
in the Gospel it is written, "Bless those that curse you, and do not evil **Matt. v. 44** *sic*
to those that do evil to you; do good to those that hate you"; be long-suffering and patient, for the Scripture saith, "Do not say, I will repay **Proverbs xx. 22** *sic*
to mine enemy evil as he has done to me, but be long-suffering, and the Lord will be a helper to thee, and will bring retribution on him that
hath done thee evil." Again He saith in the Gospel, "Love them that hate **Matt. v. 44** *sic*
you, pray for them that curse you, and no one shall be an enemy to you." Let us look therefore, O beloved, and understand these commandments, and keep them, so that we may be the children of light.

CHAPTER II.

Teaches every man that he should please his wife alone, and should not adorn himself and be a stumbling-block to women; that he should not love idleness; that he should study the Scriptures of life, and keep away from the scriptures of paganism and from the bonds which are in Deuteronomy; and that in the baths he wash not with women, and let him not give his soul to the wickedness of harlots.

Let us be patient with one another, O servants and sons of God! Let not a man despise his wife, nor behave contemptuously and haughtily towards her, but let him be compassionate, and let his hand be liberal in giving. Let him please his wife alone, and soothe her with honour; let
him study to be loved by her alone, and not by any other. Do not adorn **Ap. Con. I. iii.**
thyself so as to be seen by a strange woman and that she should desire thee. If thou, for instance, art constrained by her, and sinnest with her,

[1] S. C. Numbers.

death by fire shall come upon thee by decree from God, even that which is everlasting in the cruel and bitter fire. Thou shalt know and understand when thou art cruelly tormented. But, if thou doest not this abomination, but removest her from thee, and refusest her, in this alone thou hast sinned, that by means of thine adornment thou hast caused a woman to be held by desire of thee; for thou hast done this to her so that it has happened thus to her because of thee, and that by means of her desire she committeth adultery. But thou art not so much under sin, because thou hast not lusted after her. Mercy from the Lord shall be upon thee because thou hast not delivered thy soul unto her, and hast not been persuaded by her when she sent unto thee; not even in thy mind hast thou turned to this woman, who was held by desire of thee; but she suddenly met with thee, she was wounded in her mind, and she sent unto thee, but thou like a God-fearing man didst refuse her and remove thyself from her and hast
f. 4 a not sinned with her. She in truth was struck in her heart because thou art a youth, beautiful and good, and thou didst adorn thyself and make her desire thee. And thou art found guilty, that she hath sinned in regard to thee; for because of thine adornment it hath thus happened to her. But seek from the Lord God, that no sin may be written against thee on her account. If thou wishest to please God, and not men, and hopest for life and everlasting rest, do not adorn the beauty of thy nature which hath been given to thee by God, but with the humility of neglect, make it poor before man. Thus again also let not the hair of thy head grow, nor comb it nor dress it; but shave it, and anoint it not, that it may not attract to thee such women as snare or are snared by lust. Also wear no beautiful garments nor even put on shoes of lustful and contemptible workmanship, nor set signet-rings encased in gold upon thy fingers, because that all these things are works of harlotry, and everything that thou doest which is beyond nature. For to thee, a man who believes in God, it is not allowed to let the hair on thy head grow, to comb it and make it even, which is this voluptuousness of desire, and thou must not put it in order and dress it, nor arrange it so as to be beautiful; nor must thou destroy the hairs of thy beard, nor the likeness of the nature of thy face, nor change it to something outside of what God has created, because thou wishest to please men. If thou doest these things, thou deprivest thyself of life, and thou art rejected from the presence of
Ap. Con. I. iv. the Lord God. As a man therefore who wishes to please God, be watchful and do nothing like these things, keep away from everything which the Lord hates, and do not be wandering and turning vainly about in market-

places, seeing the inane spectacles of those who behave themselves in an evil
manner, but in thy craft and work be constant and watchful, and wishful to
do those things that are pleasing to God. Meditate constantly in the
words of the Lord. If then thou art rich and requirest not to work f. 4b
for thy livelihood, be not wandering and turning inanely about, but
be constant at all times, and have intercourse with believers and those
like-minded with thyself, and be instructed along with them in the
words of life. But if not, then stay at home, and read in the Law, Ap. Con. I.
and in the Book of the Kings and in the Prophets and in the Gospel v.
[which is] the fulness of these things. Keep far then from all the books vi.
of the heathen. For what hast thou to do with foreign words or with
false laws or prophecies, which also easily cause young people to wander
from the Faith? What then is wanting to thee in the Word of God that
thou throwest thyself upon these myths of the heathen? If thou wishest
to read the tales of the fathers, thou hast the Book of the Kings, or of
wise men and philosophers, thou hast the Prophets, amongst whom thou
wilt find more wisdom and scripture[1] than [amongst] the wise men and the
philosophers because they are the words of God, of one only wise God; if
thou desirest songs, thou hast the Psalms of David; or if the beginning
of the world, thou hast the Genesis of great Moses; if law and commandments, thou hast the Book of Exodus of the Lord our God. Therefore
keep entirely away from all these foreign things which are contrary
to them. But nevertheless what thou readest in the law of Deuteronomy, be heedful, that in reading thou readest only in it with
simplicity. From the precepts and admonitions which are in it keep well
away, lest thou lead thyself astray, and bind thyself with indissoluble heavy
chains of burdens. For this reason therefore even if thou read in
Deuteronomy, in this alone be intelligent to know, and glorify God, who
has delivered us from all these chains. Let this also be put before thine
eyes, that thou mayest distinguish and know what is the Law, and what are
the chains that are in Deuteronomy; that after the Law had been given to
those that were in the Law, on account of Deuteronomy they sinned all
these sins in the wilderness. For the Law is in the first place that which f. 5a
the Lord God spake, before the people made the calf and offered the sacrifices of idols, which is the ten Commandments and Statutes; and after they
had worshipped idols He justly put upon them chains as they deserved.
Thou therefore do not put them on thy heart, for our Saviour came for
nothing else but to fulfil the Law, and to loosen us from the chains of

[1] S. science.

Deuteronomy; for He loosened from these chains, and He called thus to
Matt. xi. 28 those who believe in Him, and said, "Come unto me all ye who are weary
and heavy laden, and I will give you rest." Thou therefore without the
weight of these burdens read the simple Law which agrees with the Gospel,
and again in the Gospel and in the Prophets, also in the Book of the Kings,
that thou mayest know how many kings were righteous, and were made
famous by the Lord God in this world, and rested also in the promises of
everlasting life. But those kings who turned aside from God, and worshipped
idols, justly perished cruelly by a decreed judgment, and were cut off from
the kingdom of God, and instead of rest they were tormented. When therefore
thou readest these things, thou shalt grow more in the faith and be increased.
After these things rise and go out to the market-place, and wash in the
baths for men, and not in those for women, lest, when thou hast stripped and
shewn the bareness and nakedness of thy body, thou wilt either be hunted
for or thou wilt constrain[1] to fall and be hunted by thee; therefore be
Ap. Con. I. vii. watchful against these things and live for God. Learn therefore what the
Prov. vii. 1 Holy Word saith in Wisdom, "My son, keep my words, and hide my commandments within thee. My son, honour the Lord and be strong, and fear
2 no other but Him; keep my commandments, and live well, and my law as
3 the apples of thine eyes, bind them on thy fingers, and write them on the
4 tables of thine heart. Say to Wisdom, Thou art my sister, and with under-
5 standing make thyself acquainted; that she may keep thee from the
6 strange woman, and the adulteress whose words are flattering; for from
7 the window of her house and her lattice she looketh out into the street,
f. 5 b and at every young man whom she seeth, those who are childish and void
8 of understanding, who pass in the streets by the side of the corners of the
9 paths of her house, and who talk in the dark, in the evening and in the
10 thick darkness of the silence of the night; then the woman goeth out, and
in the garb of a harlot she meeteth the young man, and she causeth the
11 hearts of the youths to fly away. She is rebellious and insolent and prodigal.
12 Her feet rest not in her house but she is now wandering out, and now in
13 ambush in the street and in the corners. She catcheth him who is
14 likeminded and kisseth him and maketh her face bold and saith unto him,
15 'I have peace-offerings with me, this day I have paid my vows; therefore
I have come out to meet thee, expecting to see thee, and I have found thee.
16 With a carpet have I spread my bed, and with Egyptian tapestries have
17 I covered it; I have sprinkled saffron upon my bed, and in my house there
18 is cinnamon. Come, let us enjoy ourselves with love till the morning, and

[1] S. + another.

embrace each other with desire. For my lord is not at home, he has gone 19
a long way off. He has taken a bag of silver in his hand, and he will come 20
to his house after many days.' She causeth him to err by the multitude 21
of her words, by the flattery of her lips and by a vile wink of her eyes
she draweth him unto her. He goeth after her like an infant, and like an 22
ox that goeth to the slaughter, and like a dog to the chain, and like a stag 23
which [1]an arrow pierces[1] and he fleeth, like a bird into the snare, and
he knoweth not that he is gone to the death of his soul. Wherefore 24
hearken unto me, my son, and give ear to the words of my mouth. Incline 25
not thy heart to her ways, and come not near to the door of her house; do 26
not wander in her paths; for she hath cast down a multitude of slain, her
victims are innumerable. The ways of her house are the ways of Sheol, 27
which go down to the chambers of death. My son, give ear to my wisdom, Prov. v. 1
and incline thy mind to my understanding, that my counsel may keep thee, 2
and the knowledge of my lips, which I command thee, because that 3
the lips of an adulteress distil honey, and with her flatteries she sweeteneth
the palate; yet the latter end of them is bitterer than wormwood, and 4
sharper than a two-edged-sword; for the feet of the foolish [2] woman bring 5 f. 6 a
down to the chambers of Sheol those who adhere to her, for there is
[3]nothing which goeth before[3] her heels; she walks not into the land of
life, for her paths are in error, and are not known. Therefore, my son, 6
hearken unto me, and decline not from the words of my mouth; remove 7
thy way from her, and come not near the door of her house, that thou 8
give not thy life to others, and thy years to those that have no mercy; 9
lest strangers be satisfied with thy substance, and thy merchandise [pass] 10
to the houses of others; and in thine old age thou repent thyself, when 11
the flesh of thy body faileth, and thou shalt say, Why did I hate my 12
correction and my heart reject reproof, and I did not hearken to the voice 13
of my teachers, nor incline my ears to my monitors? I was very nearly in 14
all evil things." But let us not prolong and extend the admonition of our doctrine; if we omit anything, you, like wise men, choose from what pleaseth you in the holy books, and from the Gospel of God, so that ye may be confirmed, and all these evil things may be removed and cast away from you, and ye may be found blameless in everlasting life with God.

[1] Lit. swallows an arrow. [2] S. sinful [3] S. no standing-place for

CHAPTER III.

The doctrine about women, that they please and honour their husbands only, actively and wisely, attending with diligence to the works of their houses, and that they wash not with the men nor adorn themselves, and become a cause of offence to men nor hunt after them; that they be chaste and quiet and not quarrel with their husbands.

Ap. Con. I. viii. Again, let the woman be submissive to her husband, because the head of the woman is the man, and the head of the man who walks in the way of righteousness is the Christ, after the Lord Almighty our God and the Father of the worlds, of this one which exists and of that which is to come, Lord of all breathing things and of all powers, and His living and Holy Spirit, to Whom be glory and honour for ever and ever. Amen. O woman! fear thy husband, and revere him, and please him alone; be ready for his service; stretch out thy hands to wool, and let thy mind be
Prov. xxxi. 10 on the spindle, as it is said in Wisdom, "Who can find a virtuous woman?
11 she is more precious than fine stones, which are of great value. The
12 heart of her husband doth trust in her, and treasure is not wanting to her;
she is a helper of her husband in all things; there is nothing wanting to
f. 6 b 13 him in his dwelling. She worketh wool and linen with her clever hands;
14 she furnisheth good things; like a merchant ship which gathereth all her
15 riches from afar. She riseth by night, and giveth covering to her house-
16 hold and work to her handmaids. She looketh to her field, and also buyeth
17 it, and from the fruit of her hands she planteth a possession. She girdeth
18 her loins with strength, and strengtheneth her arms. She tasteth that it is
19 good to labour; her candle goeth not out all the night. She stretcheth out
20 her arms with activity, and her hands to the spindle; she extendeth her
21 right hand to the poor, from her fruits she giveth to the needy. The master
of the house is not anxious, because that all his household is clothed with
22 wool above their raiment. She maketh for her husband garments of fine
23 linen and purple. Her husband is known in the gates, when he sitteth in
24 the seat of the elders. She maketh linen in her house, and selleth girdles
25 to the merchants. Strength and glory are her raiment, she shall rejoice
26 on the last day. She openeth her mouth in wisdom. Her tongue speaketh
27 firmly with intelligence and order; the ways of her house are strict, she
eateth not bread in idleness. She openeth her mouth according to
28 wisdom; the law of mercy is upon her tongue; her children shall arise and
grow rich, and praise her; she shall rejoice in them in the latter days; also

her husband shall call her blessed. The multitude of her daughters possess
great riches. She doeth great things and is exalted above all women,
for the woman who feareth the Lord shall be blessed. The fear of the 29
Lord is (her) glory. Give her of her fruits that are worthy of her lips. 30
She shall be honoured in the gates, and in every place her husband shall
be honoured. Again, a virtuous woman is a crown to her husband." Ye 31
have learnt therefore what praises a chaste woman who loveth her husband
receiveth from the Lord God, she who is found faithful and desirous of Prov. xii. 4
pleasing God. Therefore, thou, O chaste woman, do not adorn thyself so
as to please other men, and do not plait the plaits of harlotry, nor wear f. 7 a
the garments of lasciviousness, nor put on golden shoes, that thou mayest
be like those that are such, that thou attract not to thyself those that are
captivated by such things. Even if thou sinnest not by this act of
abomination, nevertheless in this thou sinnest, that thou obligest and
makest him to lust after thee; and if thou sinnest, thou also hast destroyed
thy life from God, and thou art guilty also concerning the soul of that
[man]. For again, as thou hast sinned with one, thou hast enervated thy
soul, and thou wilt be going also after another, as it is said in Wisdom,
"When the wicked hath gone into the depths of evil, he despiseth and ener- Prov. xviii. 3
vateth his soul; ignominy and disgrace shall come upon him." She therefore
that is thus, whose soul is completely wounded and is possessed by lust,
taketh captive the souls of those who are void of understanding. But let
us learn also about these things as the Holy Word unfolds them in
Wisdom, for it speaks thus: "As a ring of gold in a swine's snout, so is Prov. xi. 22
beauty to a woman who doeth evil": and again, "As a worm in wood, so an Prov. xii. 4 b
evil woman destroyeth a man": and again, "A woman void of understand- Prov. ix. 13
ing and boastful shall be in want of bread and shall not know shame. For 14
she sitteth in the market-place, at the door of her house on a high seat, and
she calleth to those who pass on the road and to those who walk in her ways, 15
and saith, Whoso among you is simple, let him come near to me, and he 16
who is void of understanding, and she saith to him, Come near lovingly to 17
hidden bread and to stolen waters which are sweet; and he knoweth not 18
that strong men have perished with her and have been brought to the
depths of Sheol. But flee, and tarry not in that place; do not lift thine
eyes to look at her." And again, "It is better to sit upon a turret of the Prov. xxv. 24
roof rather than to dwell with a woman who is garrulous and quarrelsome
in the middle of the house." Thou therefore who art a Christian, do not
be like such women, but if thou wishest to be faithful, please thy husband
only, and when thou walkest in the market-place, cover thy head with thy f. 7b

garment, that by thy veil the greatness of thy beauty may be covered; do not adorn the face of thine eyes, but look down and walk veiled; be watchful, not to wash in the baths with men. When there are baths for women in the city or in the district, a believing woman will not wash in the baths with men; for if thou veilest thy face from strange men by a covering of chastity, how then goest thou with strange men to the baths? But if there are no baths for women, and thou art compelled to wash in the baths for men and women, this at the least is necessary, that thou wash with chastity and modesty and bashfulness and moderation; not at every time nor every day; nor at noon, but let the time for thee to wash be known to thee, at ten o'clock; for it is required of thee, O believing woman, that by every means thou shalt flee from the multitude of vain sights of the pride of eye which is in the bath. But thy quarrel with every one, especially that with thy husband, cut short and prevent like a believing woman, lest thy husband, if he be a heathen, should be offended because of thee, and blaspheme God, and thou shouldest receive a woe from Him, for woe to those through whom the name of God is blasphemed amongst the Gentiles. Again, if thy husband be a believer, he is constrained as one who knows the Scriptures, and he will say to thee the word from Wisdom, that "it is better to dwell on a turret of the roof rather than to dwell with a garrulous and quarrelsome woman in the middle of the house." For it is required of women that by a covering of modesty and humility they show the fear of God, for the conversion and growth of the faith of those who are without, of the men and of the women. If we have a little admonished and instructed you, our sisters and daughters, our members, ye like wise women, seek and choose for yourselves those things which are excellent and honoured and without rebuke in the dwelling of the world; learn and know such things by which ye can get to the kingdom of our Lord and have rest, having already been pleasing to Him by good works.

Ap. Con. I. ix. — Ap. Con. I. x. — Rom. ii. 24 *sic* — Prov. xxv. 24 — f. 8 a

Ap. Con. II. i.

[1]*About the ordination of Bishops.* Let a Bishop be ordained having already been chosen by all the people, according to the will of the Holy Ghost, being blameless, chaste, quiet, humble, not anxious, watchful, not loving money, without accusation, not quarrelsome, clement, who does not talk excessively, a lover of good things (R.[2] + a lover of work, a lover of widows, a lover of orphans), a lover of the poor, expert in the mysteries,

[1] The remainder of Chap. III. is absent from Codex Sangerman.

[2] Rahmani, Test. D.N.J.C.

not distraught nor wandering together with the world; who is peaceable and a fulfiller of all good things, like one who is entrusted with the order and place of God. It is better that he should be and remain without a wife, Ap. Con. II. ii.
and if not, that he be husband of one wife only, that he may sympathize with the infirmity of the widows. Let him be of middle age, let him be ordained when he is not a boy. Being like this, on the Sunday let him receive the imposition of hands, all of them taking part in his ordination, and bearing witness about him with all the Elders and with all the Bishops who are near.

About the election of Elders. Let an Elder be ordained when he has the witness of all the people, like what was said before about the Bishop, wise in reading, humble, gentle, poor, not a lover of money, who has laboured much in the services of the weak, who has been proved, and is pure without a stain; if he have been a father to the orphans; if he have served the poor; if he have not stayed away from church; who in everything excels in piety; as he has been, let him be worthy in all things that have been revealed to us by God, those that are useful and those that are suitable, as those [men] are also worthy of the gifts of healing.

How it is proper for the Elder to teach, also whom, and with experience. f. 8b
Let then the teaching of the Elder be suitable and apt, gentle and temperate, mingled with reverence and fear, in the likeness also of that of the Bishop, and in the teaching let them not talk vain things, but let the hearers when they have heard all keep all, that the Elder may say, that all the things which he has taught they remember; for in the day of the Lord the word will be required which he will testify to the people, so that those may be reproved who have not obeyed; that he may rise up before the glory of the Father. Again, when he speaks the things that he is teaching, thus therefore let him teach, so that he may not perish. Let him pray for those who hear, that the Lord may give them the sense of the Spirit of the knowledge of the truth, that he may not vainly throw pearls before swine, but may prove that they are worthy who have heard and laboured, lest when the word has not brought forth fruit in them, but has perished, he may give account of its perishing.

About the election of Deacons. Let the Deacon be ordained; when he has been elected according to what has been already said, if he be of good behaviour, if he be pure, if he have been elected on account of his purity, and because of his exemption from distractions; if not thus, even if he be in wedlock with one wife; one who is witnessed of by all the believers, who is not entangled in the merchandise of the world, who does not know a

diabolical craft, who has no riches and no sons; and if he have sons[1], it is also fitting that they should cultivate the beauty of piety and that they be pure, that they may be of those who adorn the Church and the canon of service. Let the Church be careful about them so that some of them may abide permanently in the law and in the care of the service; should he not then fulfil in the church the things that are suitable? Let then the service be like this: first, those things that are commanded by the Bishop, so that they only may be done at the ministration, and of all the clergy he may be the Counsellor and secret of the Church. He who
f. 9a ministers to the sick, he who ministers to the strangers, who helps the widows, and goes round all the houses of those who are in want; lest there should be any one in distress or sickness or in misery he goes round to the houses.

About Catechumens. How he is to confirm those that are in doubt, and instruct those that are ignorant. Men who are dead he is to clothe, having adorned them, burying strangers, leading them from their dwellings, wayfarers or exiles. For the help of those who are in want let him have much care and let him inform the Church. *How it is fitting that the children of the Church should be.* Let twelve Elders be known in the Church, seven Deacons, and fourteen Subdeacons; and let those Widows who sit first be thirteen. Let the Deacon who is considered among them to be the one who is most diligent and most judicious; let him be chosen to be the receiver of strangers in the house which is the inn of the Church; let him be at all times clad in white garments, having only a *stole* upon his shoulder. In everything he is as the eye of the Church. With reverence let him make known what is to be the type of the people of piety.

The teaching of the Twelve Apostles. Behold[2] ye sons and daughters of the Church, in the name of our Lord Jesus the Christ, John, Matthew, Peter, and Philip, and Andrew, and Simeon, and James, and Jude the son of James; with Nathanael, and Thomas and Bartholomew and Matthia, all of us gathered together by command of our Lord Jesus the Christ our Saviour, according as He commanded us, that before ye are ready to divide anything by lot, for eparchies, ye shall count the places of the numbers, the authorities of the Bishops, the seats of the Elders, the continual offerings of the Deacons, the admonitions of the Readers, the blamelessnesses of the Widows, and all the things that are fitting to the foundation and confirm-

[1] Lag. *Reliquiae*, + even if he have a wife.

[2] Cod. Harris 2 and Cod. Mosul. Rejoice, Cod. H^2 + all the power of our Lord Jesus the Christ.

ation of the Church, according as they already know the type of heavenly
things. Let them take care and keep themselves from all error, knowing
that they have an account to give in the great day of judgment concerning
the things that having heard they have not kept. They commanded us
[1]to confirm[1] His words in all places. It appeared to us therefore, about the f. 9b
reminding and admonition of the brethren, that as to each one of us our
Lord revealed as the will of God by means of the Holy Ghost these words
of remembrance, we should command you. *John said*, Men, brethren,
knowing that we are about to give account concerning those things that were
commanded us, do not accept one another's persons, but if a man thinks
good to say anything that is not thine[2], let some one speak adversely to him
in opposition. It pleased them all that John should speak first. *John said*,
There are two ways, one of life and one of death, but [3]the differences are
many[3] between these two ways; for the way of life is this, first, that
thou shalt love God, Him who has made thee, with all thy heart, and
glorify Him who has redeemed thee from death, which is the first commandment. But secondly, that thou shalt love thy neighbour as thyself,
which is the second commandment, those on which hang all the Law and
the Prophets. *Matthew said*, All those things that thou dost not wish to
happen to thee, do not thou also do to others. That therefore which thou
hatest, that shalt thou not do to others. O our brother Peter, tell thou the
doctrine of these words. *Peter said*, Thou shalt not kill. Thou shalt not
commit adultery. Thou shalt not commit fornication. Thou shalt not
corrupt boys. Thou shalt not steal. Thou shalt not be a soothsayer.
Thou shalt not use enchantments. Thou shalt not kill a child at its birth,
nor after he is born shalt thou kill him. Thou shalt not covet what
belongs to thy neighbours. Thou shalt not transgress oaths. Thou shalt
not bear false witness. Thou shalt not say anything wickedly. Thou
shalt not keep anger in thy heart. Thou shalt not be double-minded, nor
double-tongued, for doubleness of tongue is a snare of death. Thy word
shall not be vain, nor false. Thou shalt not be avaricious nor rapacious.
Thou shalt not be a respecter of persons, nor evil-minded, nor be a
boaster, nor shalt thou receive evil[4] about thy neighbour; neither shalt
thou hate any one, but thou shalt reprove some, and have compassion
on others, pray for some, love others more than thyself. *Andrew
said*, My son, flee from all evil, and from all that resembles it; be not
angry, for anger leads on to murder, for anger is a masculine demon. f. 10a
Be not jealous, but peaceful; nor quarrelsome, nor irritable; for from these

[1] Cod. M. to send.
[2] S. suitable.
[3] Cod. M. there is a great difference,
[4] Rel. + counsel.

things arises murder. *Philip said,* My son, be not licentious, for lust leadeth to fornication, and attracts men towards it, for lust is a feminine demon. One with anger, the other with mirth, they destroy those into whom they enter; for the way of an evil spirit is a sin of the soul, and when it has got a little entrance, it enlarges it as itself, and brings that soul to all evil things, and does not allow the man to look and see the truth. Let there be a measure for your wrath, rule it for a little time and repress it, lest it throw you into an evil deed. For anger is an evil enjoyment, [such as] when they remain with a man for a long season, become demons, and when a man allows them, they swell up in his soul, and become greater and lead him to the works of iniquity, also they laugh at him and enjoy themselves in the destruction of the man. *Simon the Zealot said,* My son, be not a necromancer, for this will lead thee to the worship of idols; nor an enchanter, nor one who teaches extraneous and heathenish doctrine, nor an augur, nor even seek to know these things; from all these things comes the worship of idols. *James said,* My son, speak not foul and silly words, for these take one far from God, and be not haughty of eye, for every one that is haughty of eye falleth before God. Do not covet the wife of thy friend; do not love sodomy; from these things come adulteries and the wrath of God. *Nathanael said,* My son, be not false, for falsehood leads to theft, nor be a lover of money, nor vainglorious; from all these things come thefts. My son, be not a murmurer, for murmuring
f. 10b brings blasphemy, and be not proud[1] nor arrogant, nor a contriver of evil things, for from all these things come blasphemies. Therefore be meek and humble, for the meek and humble shall inherit the kingdom of Heaven; but be long suffering and merciful, a peace-maker, pure in heart from all evil, innocent, quiet, and gentle; it is good that thou shouldest attend and tremble at the words which thou hast heard. Do not exalt[2] thyself, nor set thyself with the proud, but with the righteous, and have intercourse with the poor; and the events that happen to thee receive as good things, knowing that without God nothing happens. *Thomas said,* My son, he who speaks the Word of God, and is the cause of life to thee, and gives thee the seal that is in the Christ; love him as the apple of the eye; remember him then by night and by day; honour him moreover as of God, for where the Godhead[3] is spoken of, there is the Lord. Thou shalt seek then his face daily; also the other Saints, that thou mayest be soothed by their words; for thou being joined to the Saints, art sanctified. Thou shalt honour him then as thou art able, by thy sweat and by the labour of thy hands. For if through him the Lord has

[1] C. rich. [2] C. love. [3] lit. Lordship.

honoured thee by giving thee spiritual food and the water of everlasting life, much more must thou offer him perishable and temporal food, for the labourer is worthy of his hire. The ox that grinds thou shalt not muzzle; and no one planteth a vineyard, and eateth not of its fruit. *Jude the son of James*[1] *said*, My son, do not make schisms; calm those who are quarrelling, and judge righteously. Be no respecter of persons in reproving a man who is in fault, for riches can have no power with the Lord, nor does the Lord give more honour to dignities, nor has beauty any advantage, but there is equality of all these things with Him. In thy prayer do not doubt which of them shall be yea or nay. Let it not be that thou shouldest stretch out thine hand in order to receive, whilst[2] the hand that giveth thou contractest[2]. If there be [aught] f. 11 a in thy hands, give the redemption of thy sins, and do not hesitate to give, nor when thou givest murmur and tell. Know then who is the good payer of thy reward. Turn not thy face from the needy; share with thy brother in all things, and say not that they are thine own, for if ye are sharers in immortal things how much more in those that are perishable? *Bartholomew said*, We then persuade you, my brethren, that while it is yet time, and whilst ye have among you some of the things by which ye work, ye should not spare yourselves in anything whatever of what ye have, for the day of the Lord is at hand in which all these things will be destroyed together with the Wicked One. For our Lord shall come, and His reward with Him. To yourselves then be lawgivers; be good counsellors of yourselves, taught of God. Keep these things that thou hast received, not adding to them, and also not diminishing from them.

Matthia[3] *said about the Readers.* Let a Reader be appointed, having first been proved by many probations, not a talkative man, not a drunkard, not a speaker of laughable things; of good manner, of good disposition, persuadable, of good will; who in the Lord's congregations on Sundays runs first, good at hearing, and as a maker of narratives; who knows that he takes the place of an Evangelist.

Cod. Harris 2. *Peter said*, Brethren, other things concerning admonition the Scriptures teach, but let us command and teach the things that we have been commanded.

All of them said, Let Peter speak.

Peter said, If there be (M + few people in a place,) and not many (M + such as can make choice about a Bishop, nearly twelve men, let them write to those Churches that are near, where there is a Church founded, so that from thence

[1] C. M. + Cephas. [2] C. with the hand that giveth thou castest lots.

[3] In the Mosul Codex this speech is given to James, and comes somewhat later, after that of John, p. 16.

may come three chosen and tried men, to prove him who is worthy; if he be a man who has a good report from the Gentiles; if he be without sin, if he be not irascible, if he be a lover of the poor, if he be chaste, if he be not a drunkard, nor a fornicator, not avaricious, nor a calumniator, nor a respecter of persons, nor anything like these. It is a good thing if he have no wife, or if not, that he have one wife; who is a sharer in discipline, who is able to explain the Scriptures, but if he know not letters, let him be meek and humble, and in love to all men let him abound, lest he be reproved about anything by the masses, let him be a Bishop.

John said, Let the Bishop who is appointed, knowing the diligence and the love of God, and those who are with him, appoint two Elders, those whom he has proven.

All of them objected to this, and said, Not two, but three, for there are twenty-four Elders, twelve on the right hand and twelve on the left.

John said, Well do ye remember, my Brethren, for those on the right hand are those who having received (M. + the vials) from the Archangels instead of a reward, which they offer to the Lord, but those on the left rule over many angels. It is right that there should be Elders, those who formerly were for some time removed from the world, and in some way removed from intercourse with women, good at giving to the brethren, who do not accept any man's person, sons of the Mystery of the Bishop, and his assistants in gathering the people together, who act promptly with the Pastor and serve him. Let the Elders who are on the right have the care of those who labour at the altar, so that they may give honour and blame, and may reprove in what is necessary. But let the Elders who are at the left have the care of the multitude of the people, so that there be good administration without tumult, they having learnt beforehand to conduct themselves with all submission. But if a man, having been admonished, give an answer (M. rebelliously), those who are at the altar, being of one opinion, shall judge him that is such with one mind, as he deserves, so that the others also may fear, lest they accept one another's persons, and many think evil with the evildoers, and the evil spread like a gangrene, and all be taken captive.

James said (as Mathia on p. 15). He that fills the ears of him that is ignorant of what is written is considered before God.

Matthew said, Let three Deacons be appointed, for it is written that in the mouth of two or three every word of the Lord shall be established. Let them be those who are proved in all their service, that they may have witness from strangers and from the congregation, that they are [but once] married[1], and that their children are chaste, gentle, peaceable, not grumblers, not double-tongued, not wrathful, for wrath destroyeth a wise man; not respecters of the persons of the rich, nor oppressing the poor; not using much wine, very laborious and inventive in works that are hidden and good; inciters, obliging and constraining those of the brethren who have aught to stretch out their hands to give, and let them also be good givers, and communicators, that they may be honoured by the people with all possible honour and reverence, watching carefully for those who walk disorderly, dealing tenderly with some of them, and persuading others, inciting others with reproof, and others, who show complete contempt, excommunicating, knowing that those who are quarrelsome and contemptuous, and calumniators, are depraved, opposing themselves to the Christ.

Cephas said, Let three Widows be appointed, two who shall be continually in

[1] Cod. unmarried.

prayer for all those who are in temptation and in regard to revelations and signs, for what is necessary, but one to be continually with the women who are tried by sickness, who is good at service, watchful to make known what is required to the Elders. [Let them] not be lovers of filthy lucre, not accustomed to much wine, so that they may be able to be watchful in the night services of the sick, and in any other good works that any one wishes to do, for these things are the first good treasures [1]that are desirable[1]. *Andrew said*, Let Deacons, doers of good works, go round to every place by night and by day, that they may not neglect the poor, nor accept the persons of the rich; let them recognize him who is in straits, and deprive him not of the blessings. Let them constrain those who are able to lay up for themselves treasures in good works, looking forward to the words of our Teacher, that ye saw Me hungry, and fed Me not; for those who have served Him well and blamelessly, prepare for themselves [2]a large place[2].

Philip said, The laymen shall obey the commands for laymen, being submissive to those who serve continually at the altar. Every one in his place shall please the Lord, not shewing enmity to one another concerning those things that are appointed, every one in that wherein he has been called of God. Let not one persuade to the course of another, for the angels also, beyond what is appointed to them, do no other things.

Andrew said, It would be very good, my brethren, that we should appoint women as Deaconesses.

Peter said, As we have commanded and appointed all these things, and arrived at this point, let us in truth make known accurately about the offerings of the Body and Blood.

John said, It has escaped you, my brethren, that when our Teacher asked for the Bread and the Cup, and blessed them saying, This is my Body and my Blood, He did not allow these to remain with us.

Martha said about Mary, I saw her laughing between her teeth joyfully.

Mary said, I did not surely laugh, but I remembered the words of our Lord, and I rejoiced, for ye know that He said to us before, when He was teaching, He that is weak shall be saved by means of the strong.

Cephas said, We ought to remember the single things, for it is not fitting for women to take the communion with heads uncovered, but having covered their heads.

James said, How then can we define any service for the women, except only some service of strengthening and helping those women who are in want?

Philip said, Now, my brethren, let us say this to you, in regard to the participation in gifts. He that doeth good works, lays up and prepares good treasures for himself, for he who lays up for himself treasures in the kingdom shall be counted as a workman (it is written) before God.

Peter said, These things, my brother, we do not command as necessary from the power that we have over men, but as we have a commandment from the Lord, our Lord, we persuade you to keep the commandments, not diminishing aught from them nor adding aught.

In the name of our Lord Jesus the Christ, to whom be glory for ever and ever. Amen.

The teaching of the Twelve holy Apostles is finished by the hands of Baltous, an odious and lazy servant of the Christ, son of George Moses of the tribe of the

[1] M. of the Lord. [2] M. the place of a shepherd.

household of John, from the village of the fortress of the woman, which is beside the Convent of Kourkama, an (episcopal) see of Western Syria, between the city of Mardin and the above-mentioned Convent in the year 1896 in the month of July, and to Him be glory, may His mercies be over us for ever.

From Paul the Apostle about the Times of Prayer. Institute prayer in the morning and at the third hour, and at the sixth hour, and at the ninth hour, and in the evening, and when ye go to sleep, that for protection, and at the cockcrow: in the morning thanking God who has given us light, having made the night to pass and brought the day; at the third hour because at it our Lord suffered judgment from Pilate;
f. 11 b in that of the sixth hour because in it the Christ was crucified, all created things were shaken, trembling at the daring deed which the wicked Jews did; He was pierced in His side by a lance, and shed forth blood and water; in that of the ninth hour because when our Lord was crucified the sun was darkened at mid-day, and the dead arose from their graves; created things could not bear to see the ignominy of our Lord; also He gave up His Spirit into the hands of His Father; in that of the evening thanking God, who gave us the night for rest from the labours of the day; in that for protection while ye now slumber the sleep of rest from work; but pray that in sleep and in rest ye leave not this world, and if that should happen, the prayer which ye have prayed will help you in the way that is everlasting; and at cockcrow, because that is the hour in which announcement is made to us of the coming of the day, and for the labour of the works of light.

Commandments from the writing of Addai the Apostle.

(1) The Holy Apostles have therefore decreed, first, that people should pray towards the East, because, that as the lightning that flashes from the East, and is seen unto the West, thus shall be the coming of the Son of Man. By this let us know and understand when we pray, that He shall be seen from the East, and towards it we expect Him and we worship Him.

(2) Again, the Apostles have decreed, that on Sunday there shall be service and reading of the Holy Scriptures, and the Eucharist, because that on Sunday the Christ rose from the dead, and on Sunday He ascended to Heaven; on Sunday again He will appear at the end with His holy Angels.

(3) Again, the Apostles have decreed that on Wednesday there shall be service, that is to say, the Eucharist, because that on it our Lord revealed to His Apostles about His judgment and passion, and crucifixion, and death, and resurrection; and the disciples were in sorrow about this.

(4) Again, the Apostles have decreed, that also on Friday at the

ninth hour there shall be service, because of what was said on Wednesday about the Passion of our Saviour; on the Friday it was accomplished, the earth quaking and all creatures crying out, and the lights in the heaven were darkened. f. 12a

(5) The Apostles have also decreed that there shall be Elders in the Church like the holy Priests, the sons of Aaron; and Deacons, like the Levites; and Subdeacons, like those who carried the vessels of the court of the sanctuary of the Lord; and an Overseer who should be leader of all the people, like Aaron the High Priest, chief and leader of all the Levites and priests and of all the camp.

(6) The Apostles have also decreed that they should make the day of the Epiphany of our Saviour to be the beginning of the yearly feasts, on the 6th of January (second Conun) according to the number of the months of the Greeks.

(7) The Apostles have also decreed that forty days before the Passion of our Saviour they should fast, and then should keep the day of His Passion and the day of His Resurrection, because that also our Lord Himself, the Lord of the feast, fasted for forty days; also Moses and Elias, who were clothed with this mystery, fasted for forty days and then were glorified.

(8) The Apostles have also decreed that at the end of all the Scriptures the Gospel shall be read as the seal of all the Scriptures, the people rising to their feet to hear it; because it is the Message of the Salvation of all men.

(9) The Apostles have also decreed that at the end of forty days after His Resurrection, they should make remembrance of His Ascension to His glorious Father.

(10) The Apostles have also decreed that except the Old (Testament) and the Prophets, and the Gospel, and the Acts of their own triumphs, nothing should be read from the pulpit in the Church.

(11) The Apostles have also decreed that he who does not know the faith of the Church and the ordinances and the laws that are decreed in it, shall not be a leader and commander; and he who knows them and transgresses them, shall not again serve; because he is not true in his service, but false.

(12) The Apostles have also decreed that he who swears and is untrue, f. 12b or who bears false witness or goes with wizards and diviners and Chaldæans, and confirms fortunes and nativities, or anything which those who know not God hold to; as if he were a man who knows not God, let him be put out of His service, and never again serve in it.

(13) The Apostles have also decreed that if there be a man who is doubtful about his service and not sure of it, he shall never again serve, because the Lord of the service is not real to him, and he deceives men;
Cf. 1 Sam. ii. 3. but not God, before whom stratagems are not established.

(14) The Apostles have also decreed that he who lends and takes usury, or he who uses merchandise of avarice, shall never again serve, and shall not remain in his service.

(15) The Apostles have also decreed that he who loves the Jews like Judas Iscariot who loved them, or the heathen, who worship the creatures instead of the Creator, shall not enter among them nor serve; or if he be among them, they shall not allow him, but he shall be separated from them, and shall not serve with them.

(16) The Apostles have also decreed that if there have come a man of the Jews or of the heathen and been mingled with them, and after he has come and has been received and mingled with them, he have turned and gone again to the sect in which he stood, and again have come and been converted to them for the second time, he shall not be received again, but as the sect in which he was at the first, thus those that know him shall regard him.

(17) The Apostles have also decreed that it shall not be lawful for the ruler to administer the affairs of the Church without those who serve along with him, but in the counsel of all he shall command and oversee that with which all shall be pleased, and not in any way oppressed.

f. 13a (18) The Apostles have also decreed that all those who go out of this world in the martyrdom of the faith of Jesus the Christ, and in tribulation for His Name's sake, of them remembrance shall be made on the day of their murders.

(19) The Apostles have also decreed that whilst they stand in the service of the Church, they should recite the songs of David every day;
Ps. xxxiv. 1 because of this, "I will bless the Lord at all times, and at all times His songs
Ps. lv. 17 are in my mouth," and "in the night I will meditate and say and cause my voice to be heard before Thee."

(20) The Apostles have also decreed that those who are void of riches and do not run after increase of silver shall be chosen and also presented for the service of government.

(21) The Apostles have also decreed that the priest who binds in a hap-hazard and unjust manner shall receive punishment justly; but he who is bound shall receive the interdict as he who is reasonably bound.

(22) The Apostles have also decreed that those who are accustomed

to hear judgment, if it be perceived that they are respecters of persons condemning the innocent, and acquitting the guilty; they shall not again hear another judgment, and they shall also receive the reproof of their partiality.

(23) The Apostles have also decreed that those who are high-minded and lifted up in the haughtiness of pride shall not be presented for service, because of this that "he who is haughty among men is abominable before God," for it is also said, "I will repay vengeance on them that exalt themselves." **Luke xvi. 15** **Ps. xxxi. 23**

(24) The Apostles have also decreed that the commands of the Bishop shall be upon the Elders of the Churches who are in all the villages, that he may be known to be the chief of them all, that through him they may all be judged, for Samuel also visited thus from place to place and commanded. f. 13b

(25) The Apostles have also decreed that those kings who shall become believers in the Christ; it shall be lawful for them to go up and stand before the altar with the Ruler of the Church, because also David and those who were like him went up and stood before the altar of the Lord.

(26) The Apostles have also decreed that no man shall venture to do anything with the authority of the priesthood in unrighteousness and impropriety but in integrity without accusation of partiality.

(27) The Apostles have also decreed that the bread of the Eucharist in the day in which it is cooked shall be [1]laid on the altar[1], and not after some days, which is not lawful.

Again, a little of the Canons of the Apostles, and the Fathers, by which the Church of the Christ is truly bound. To those who in everything agree with us in the Orthodox faith, and in the Apostolic laws; the holy Bishops, the glorious Priests, the pure Deacons; and the faithful and Christ-loving people, with the rest of all the ecclesiastical order, and the sons of the Lord; who live, that is to say, dwell as strangers in all the various provinces, keeping (themselves) continually in the Lord, Amen...Because, therefore, O beloved, we are sons and heirs of the laws, prophetical and apostolic, those which command and warn us that continually and always we shall learn the way which is straight and good, and that we should go in it; we have appointed to you twenty Canons, and they are these.

Canon I. A man shall not take a wife, and his son her daughter.

II. Nor shall a man take a girl, and his son the mother of the girl.

[1] Cod. consumed as bread.

III. Nor a man and his son two sisters, or two daughters of a paternal uncle.

IV. Nor two brothers a woman and her daughter.

V. Also a man shall not take a woman, and give his daughter to her son.

f. 14a VI. Nor a man a woman, and give his daughter to her brother.

VII. Nor a man a woman, and give his daughter to her father.

VIII. Nor shall a man take the sister of his wife nor the daughter of his sister.

IX. Nor a man the wife of the brother of his wife.

X. Nor the wife of a brother or the wife of his son.

XI. Nor (is) a man bound to the wife of his paternal uncle.

XII. Nor is the wife of a mother's brother lawful.

XIII. Nor let a man take the daughter of the brother of his wife.

XIV. Nor let a man take his godmother from among men for three generations.

XV. Nor the brothers of that one for two generations.

XVI. Nor let a man take a (fellow-) sponsor of baptism, nor a man who is related to him in race for five generations.

XVII. Nor let an Elder baptize his son according to the flesh, unless a reason of death should happen to that child and there be no stranger Elder to baptize him.

XVIII. Nor let a man confirm the espousals of a woman except before the Elders and Deacons, and before free persons who are worthy to be believed.

XIX. And he who espouses a spouse let him not do violence to the girl, and let him not see her face until he has fulfilled to her all (things) that are obligatory to the order of Christians, and let the girl enter his house.

XX. It is not lawful for a Christian to give a woman to any kind of marriage with a Nestorian or with a people out of our fold, nor to a heretic, nor to those who are strange to us in faith.

These things we have determined thus and appointed to you as to sons and obedient people; as therefore ye keep them and walk in them, attend also to the Canons spoken by the Spirit; by them ye shall be kept, in this world ye shall be blest, and in that which is to come ye shall be saved to the kingdom of our Lord and ye shall have rest, pleasing Him by good works.

CHAPTER IV.

Teaches what sort of man it is right to be chosen for the Bishopric, and what like his works should be.

About Bishops hear thus. Of the Pastor who is appointed as a Bishop Ap. Con. II. i.
and chief in the Eldership of the Church in all the assemblies, it is required f. 14 b
that he be without reproof, irreprehensible, that he be far from all evil things,
a man who is not less than fifty years (of age) and therefore far from the
vehement manners of youth, from the desires of the Enemy, and from
calumny, and from the blasphemy of false brethren which they bring against
many, because they do not understand the word which is spoken in the
Gospel, that "every one who speaks an idle word shall give account of Matt. xii. 36
it to the Lord in the day of judgment, for by thy words thou shalt be 37
justified, and by thy words thou shalt be condemned." If it be possible
let him be a teacher, and if he be illiterate, let him be persuasive and
wise of speech: let him be advanced in years. If the assembly be small
and there be not found a man advanced in years, [one] about whom there
be witnesses that he is wise and suitable to be appointed Bishop; one being
found who is a youth, whose companions testify about him, and those who are
with him, that he is worthy to be appointed to the Bishopric; he though
yet a youth shewing the works of age in humility and meekness, if all men
testify about him, being proved by all the people; thus let him sit in peace,
because that even King Solomon when twelve years of age, reigned over
Israel, and Josiah reigned in righteousness when eight years of age; again
also Joash, when seven years of age, reigned over Israel; therefore, this
man even if he be a youth, yet let him be meek and reverent and
gentle; because the Lord God said by Isaiah, "To whom will I look and Is. lxvi. 2
with [whom] will I rest, but with the gentle and meek who trembleth *sic*
at My words"...Also in the Gospel He saith thus, "Blessed are the Matt. v. 5
meek, for they shall inherit the earth"; and let him be merciful, for He
saith in the Gospel, "Blessed are the merciful, for on them shall be mercy"; 7
and again, let him be a peacemaker, for it is said, "Blessed are the peace- 9 f. 15 a
makers, for they shall be called the children of God." Let him be pure
from all evil things, and injustice and iniquity, for it is said, "Blessed are Matt. v. 8
the pure in heart, for they shall see God." Let him be watchful, and chaste, Ap. Con. II. ii.
and stable, and well-regulated, and let him not be turbulent, nor trespass

in wine, nor be a calumniator, nor let him be contentious, nor a lover
of money, nor have a childish mind, nor let him exalt himself and fall into
Luke xiv. 11 the condemnation of Satan; for it is said that, "every one that exalteth
himself shall be abased." Thus the Bishop is required to be; a man who
has taken one wife, who ruleth his house well; and thus let him be proved
when he receives the laying on of hands, that he may sit in the place of the
Bishops, if he be chaste, and if also his wife be believing and chaste, and
if he have brought up his children in the fear of God, and if he have
admonished and taught them, and if they reverence and respect him at
home, and if all of them be obedient to him; for if his household
according to the flesh oppose him and do not obey him, how shall those
Ap. Con. II. iii. who are without belong to him and submit to him? Let it also be proved
that he is blameless in the affairs of the world, and in his body, for it is
Lev. xxi. 17 written; "See that there be no blemish in him who is appointed priest."
Prov. xv. 1 Let him be also without anger, for the Lord hath said that anger destroyeth
1 Peter iv. 8 even the wise. Let him be merciful and gracious and full of love, for the
Lord hath said that love shall cover a multitude of sins. Let his hand be
stretched out to give; let him love both orphans and widows. Let him
love the poor, and also strangers. Let him be apt in his service, and let
him be constant in service. Let him humble himself, and not be ashamed;
Ap. Con. II. iv. let him know who is most worthy to receive. For if there be a widow who
f. 15 b possesses aught, or if she be able to provide for herself anything that is
necessary for the nourishment of the flesh; and if there be another who is
not yet a widow and is in want, either on account of sickness or the education of children, or because of the infirmity of the flesh, to this one rather
let him stretch out his hand. If there be a person, who is spendthrift or
drunken or lazy, and is constrained in provision for the flesh, this one is
not worthy of alms nor even for the Church. Therefore let the Bishop also
Ap. Con. II. v. not be a respecter of persons, and let him not be ashamed before the rich,
and let him not please them beyond what is right, and let him not despise
or neglect the poor; let him not be haughty towards them. Let him be
frugal and poor in his food and drink; so that he can be watchful in
admonition and in discipline towards those who have no education. Let
him not be very designing nor eccentric, nor be luxurious, nor let him love
dainties, nor love pleasant viands, and let him not be irritable, but let him
be long-suffering in his admonition. Let him be very diligent in his
instruction; let him be constant in the reading of the divine books
assiduously, that he may interpret and explain the Scriptures accurately.
Let him compare the Law and the Prophets with the Gospel, how that the

commandments of the Law and the Prophets agree with the Gospel. Before all things then let him be a good discriminator of the Law, and of Deuteronomy, so that he may distinguish and shew what is the law of believers, and what are the chains of the unbelievers; lest any man of those who are under thy hand should take the chains to be the Law, and should put heavy
burdens upon his soul, and should become a son of perdition. Be therefore f. 16a
diligent and careful about the Word, O Bishop, if thou [1]canst explain[1] every commandment as it is in the doctrine.

(Cod. S. in order that by much teaching, thou mayest abundantly nourish and
water thy people, for it is written in Wisdom, "Take care of the herb of the field, Prov.
and shear thy flock; and gather the grass of summer, that there may be sheep for thy xxvii. 25
clothing. Take care and attend to thy flock, so that thou mayest have lambs." There- 26
fore let not the Bishop love filthy lucre, especially not from the heathen; let him be oppressed and not be an oppressor, and let him not love riches, and let him not murmur at any one, and do not let him bear false witness, nor be wrathful, nor let him love disputes, nor let him love rule; let him not be double-minded, nor double-tongued; and let him not love to incline his ear to the words of an accuser and a murmurer, and let him not be a respecter of persons.)

Let him not love heathen feasts, nor be led by vain error. Let him Ap. Con.
not be covetous, nor love money, because all these things come from II. vi.
the operation of demons. Then let the Bishop inquire into all these things and warn the whole world. Let him be wise and self-denying. Let him be a monitor and a teacher in his doctrine and in the discipline of God. Let his mind be clear, let him be far from all wicked designs of the heathen; let his mind be sharp to compare, that he may anticipate and know the wicked, and ye may keep yourselves from them. Let him be a lover of all men, being a righteous judge. Everything that is found good among men, let these things be in the Bishop; because when the pastor is far from all evil things, he can also constrain his disciples, and encourage them by his good manners, that they may be imitators of his good works;
as the Lord said in the Twelve Prophets, "let the people be like the Hos. iv. 9
priest"; for it is required of you that ye be an example to the people, for ye also have the example of the Christ. Therefore be ye also a good example to your people. For the Lord has said in Ezekiel the Prophet,
"The word of the Lord was upon me, saying, Son of man, speak to the Ezekiel
children of thy people, and say unto them, The land, when I bring a xxxiii. 2
sword upon it, and captivity upon the people of this land, and they appoint
a man from among them and make him a watchman, and he seeth the 3
sword coming upon the land, and he bloweth with the trumpet and warneth 4

[1] Cod. canst not explain.

the people; and whosoever heareth the sound of the trumpet and taketh
f. 16b not warning, and the sword cometh and taketh him away, his blood shall
5 be upon his head, because he heard the sound of the trumpet, and took
not warning, his blood shall be upon his head, but he that taketh warning
6 shall deliver his soul. But if the watchman see the sword coming, and
blow not the trumpet, and warn not the people, and the sword come
and take any soul from among them, he shall be taken away in his sins,
but his blood shall be required at the watchman's hands." Therefore the
sword is the judgment and the trumpet is the Gospel; the watchman is
the Bishop who is appointed over the Church.

CHAPTER V.

Doctrine and caution for the Bishop, that he should preach about judgment and warn the people, and remove himself from the disobedient, and judge those who do wrong like God, and not spare those that are wicked, and corrupt the people. It is required of thee, therefore, O Bishop,
that when thou preachest thou shouldst testify and affirm about judgment,
Ezekiel xxxiii. 7 as in the Gospel, because the Lord hath said also to thee, "Also thou, O
son of man, I have set thee for a watchman unto the house of Israel, that
thou mayest hear the word at My mouth, and take heed, and preach it as
8 from Me. When I say unto the wicked, That the wicked shall surely die,
and thou dost not preach and say, so that the wicked may turn from his
iniquity, the wicked man shall die in his iniquity, but his blood will I
9 require at thy hands. But thou, if thou warn the people from its way and
it be not warned, the wicked shall die in his iniquity, but thou shalt deliver
thy soul." Therefore ye also, because upon you will fall the accusation of those who have sinned without knowing, preach and testify, and those who walk without discipline, admonish and reprove them publicly. Though we say and repeat these things often, O brethren, let us not be blamed, for by a great deal of doctrine and by much hearing it may happen that a man is made to blush, and to do good things and avoid evil things. For
Deut. vi. 4 the Lord saith in the Law, "Hear, O Israel," and to this day he has not
f. 17a heard. Again, in the Gospel he preacheth much and saith, "Every one
Matt. xi. 15 that hath ears to hear, let him hear," and they have not heard, even those
that thought they heard, because they leaned to the evil perdition of the
Ap. Con. II. vii. heresies, those on whom the sentence of condemnation will come, for we
do not believe, brethren, that when a man goeth down to the water, he will again do the abominable and impure works of the heathen and the depraved;

for this is manifest and known to all men, that every one who doeth evil
things after having received baptism, is already condemned to the Gehenna
of fire. We think that even the heathen blaspheme on account of these Ap. Con. II. viii.
things, because we do not mix with them, nor are we partakers with them;
and by means of the falseness of the heathen, keep the more, brethren, to
the truth; for He saith thus in the Gospel, "Blessed are ye when they Matt. v. 11
shall revile you, and shall say against you every evil word falsely for my
sake; rejoice then and be glad, for great is your reward in Heaven, for 12
thus your fathers persecuted the prophets." Therefore if they blaspheme
against a man falsely he is blessed, because he is tried by temptations,
saith the Lord. And the Scripture saith, A man who is not tried is also
not proved. For if a man be reproved for doing wicked works, he is not
a Christian, but is false, and by hypocrisy he has adhered to the worship of
God. On this account when some of these are detected and reproved in
truth publicly, let the Bishop reject them, he who is without offence and
without hypocrisy. If then even his mind be not pure, having respect to Ap. Con. II. ix.
persons on account of filthy lucre, or on account of the presents he has
received, and he should spare him who has sinned wickedly [and] allow him x.
to remain in the Church, the Bishop who is such pollutes the congregation
before God, and also before men, and before many of the communicants
who are young in their minds, or before the hearers; again also he destroys f. 17 b
those that are young along with himself; for on account of the wicked
lasciviousness which they saw in him among them, they also doubt in
their souls, and imitate him, and they also stumble and are taken by this
passion and perish with him....But if he who sinneth see the Bishop
and the Deacons, that they are free from accusation and that all the flock
are pure, in the first place he will not dare to go up to the congregation
because he is reproved by his mind; and if it should happen that he
have courage, and should go to the church in his impudence, let him be
reproved and reprimanded by the Bishop; he will look at them all, and
will not find an offence in one of them, neither in the Bishop, nor
in those who are with him; he will blush therefore, and with much
shame he will go out quickly, weeping, and be in penitence of soul.
Thus the flock will remain pure. Again, when he has gone out he will
repent of his sin and weep and be consoled before God, that he may have
hope. Then again, all the flock, having seen his weeping and his tears, will
fear, knowing and understanding that every one that sins shall perish.
Because of this, therefore, O Bishop, strive to be pure in thy works, and Ap. Con. II. xi.
know thy place, that thou art appointed in the semblance of God Almighty,

and that thou holdest the place of God Almighty; thus sit in the Church
and teach, as one who hath power to judge those that sin, in the place of
Matt. xviii. 18 Almighty God; for to you Bishops it is said in the Gospel, that what ye
bind on earth shall be bound in Heaven.

CHAPTER VI.

*Also teaches the Bishop, that he judge him that sins, as God, and not
spare him; that he receive in love him that repents and pardon him, and that
f. 18 a he adhere not to the passions of the laity, and shut the door in the face of those
who repent, but according to the greatness of his honour he carry the burden
of all men's sins; with demonstration and threatening from Ezekiel, about
Bishops who despise their flocks or about laymen who contemn the Bishop.*
Ap. Con. II. xii. Therefore judge severely, O Bishop, like Almighty God, and receive those
who repent with compassion like God; and reprove, and beseech and
teach, for even the Lord God has promised with oaths pardon to those
Ezekiel xxxiii. 10 who have sinned, as Ezekiel the prophet has said, "And thou, son of
man, say to them of the house of Israel; Thus ye say, our transgressions
and our sins are upon us, and in them we pine away; how should we then
11 live? Say unto them, As I live, saith the Lord God, I do not wish the
death of the sinner, but that the wicked should repent of his evil way and
live; repent therefore and turn from your evil deeds, and ye shall not die,
ye house of Israel." Here therefore he gives hope to those who have sinned
when they repent, that they may have forgiveness in their repentance;
and their hope may not be cut off, and that they may not remain in
their sins, nor add to these; but that they may repent and weep for
Ap. Con. II. xiii. their sins, and be converted with all their heart; and those who have not
sinned may remain without sins; lest these also should have need of
weeping and sighings and forgiveness. How knowest thou, O man that
hath sinned, how many may be the days of thy life in this world that thou
mayest repent, for thou knowest not thy departure from this world; lest
thou shouldest die in thy sins and have no repentance, as it is said in
Psalm vi. 5 David, "In Sheol who confesseth to Thee?" Therefore every one who
hath pity on himself and remaineth without sins, may remain without
f. 18 b danger; so that the righteousness which was done by him of old may be
Ap. Con. II. xiv. kept for him. Thou therefore, O Bishop, judge thus, first severely, and
afterwards receive with mercy and clemency [him who] has promised to
repent, reprove him and make him sorry and persuade him, because of the
Ps. lxxiv. 19 word that was said in David thus, "Thou wilt not give up the soul of him

that confessseth to Thee." Again, in Jeremiah He saith thus, about the
repentance of those that sin, " He that falleth, shall he not rise; or he that Jer. viii. 4
turneth away [shall he] not turn back? Why hath My people turned away 5
with a shameless turning; they are held fast in their thoughts, and do not
wish to repent and be converted." Because of this therefore receive him who
repenteth, not doubting in the least, and be not prevented by those who have
no mercy, those who say, We must not be defiled by those. For the Lord
God hath said, "The fathers shall not die for the children, nor the children 2 Chron. xxv. 4
for the fathers." And again in Ezekiel he saith thus, "The word of the Lord Ezek. xiv. 13
came unto me, saying, Son of man, when a land sinneth against Me, and
doeth wickedness before Me, I will stretch out My hand against it, and
I will destroy from it the staff of bread, and I will send famine upon it,
and I will destroy from it man and beast. Though these three men were 14
in it, Noah, and Daniel, and Job, they should deliver their souls by their
righteousness, saith the Lord God." The Scripture therefore plainly sheweth
that if the righteous be found with the wicked, he will not perish with him,
but every man shall live by his righteousness, and if he be prevented, he is
prevented by his own sins. In Wisdom again He saith, "Every man is bound Prov. v. 22
with the cord of his sins." Every one of the laity therefore shall give an
account of his own sin and no man will be hurt because of the foreign
sins of others. Not even Judas did cause us any loss by praying with f. 19a
us, but he alone perished. Noah also in the Ark and two of his sons
who were saved, were blessed; but Ham, the other, was not blessed; but
his seed was cursed, [1]because he mocked at his father, for going out to the
beasts[1]. We do not require you therefore to confirm[2] those who delight
in death, hate their brethren, and love quarrels, for which reason they
are ready to kill; but help those who are very sick, and are in danger
and sin, and deliver them from death, not according to the hardness of
their heart and their word and [3]their thoughts[3]. For it is not required
of thee, O Bishop, that being the head thou shouldst listen to the tail,
that is to say, to the layman, to the quarrelsome man who delights in
the destruction of another; but look thou only at the command of the
Lord God, and for this reason, that they may not expect to perish, nor be
defiled with the sins of others. Cut away also their evil thoughts. Even
in Ezekiel the Lord God saith thus, "The word of the Lord came unto Ezek. xviii. 1
me, saying, Son of man, why use ye this proverb in the land of Israel, 2
saying, The fathers have eaten sour grapes, and the children's teeth are set

[1] S. for he who came in as beast went out as beast.

[2] S. obey. [3] S. the thoughts of men.

3 on edge. As I live, saith the Lord God, ye shall not use this proverb any
4 more in Israel, because all souls are mine; the soul of the father is mine,
thus also the soul of the son is mine; the soul that sinneth, it shall die.
5, 6 If a man be righteous, and doeth judgment and righteousness, and
eateth not upon the mountains, and lifteth not up his eyes to the idols
of the house of Israel, and defileth not his neighbour's wife, and cometh
7 not near to a woman in her separation, and hath not acted to any one with
f. 19 b violence, and even returneth the pledge of the debtor which he hath taken,
8 and clotheth the naked with a garment, and giveth not out his money to
usury, and taketh not with avarice, and withdraweth his hand from iniquity,
9 and judgeth true judgment between man and man, and walketh in my laws,
and doeth my statutes and keepeth them; this is a righteous man, he shall
10 surely live, saith the Lord God. If he beget an evil son who sheddeth
blood and doeth murder, and walketh not in the way of his righteous
11 father, and eateth on the mountains, and defileth his neighbour's wife, and
12 oppresseth the poor and needy, robbeth with violence, and returneth not
the pledge that he hath taken; lifteth up his eyes to the idols, doeth
13 iniquity, giveth out his money to usury, and taketh with avarice, he shall
not live, because he hath done all this iniquity, he shall surely die, and his
14 blood shall be upon him. Now if he beget a son, and he seeth all these
sins that his father hath done, and feareth, and doeth not like unto him;
15 and eateth not upon the mountains, and lifteth not up his eyes to the idols
16 of the house of Israel, and defileth not his neighbour's wife, and oppresseth
no man, and taketh no pledge, and robbeth not with violence; and giveth
17 his bread to the hungry, and clotheth the naked with a garment, and
withdraweth his hand from iniquity, and taketh not usury and avaricious
gain, and doeth righteousness, and walketh in My laws, he shall not die in
18 the iniquity of his father, but he shall surely live. But his father, because
he hath grievously oppressed, and robbed with violence, and hath not done
19 good to My people, he shall die in his iniquity. And ye say, Why is not
the son punished for the iniquity of his father? because the son hath done
righteousness and mercy, and hath kept all My commandments and done
20 them, he shall surely live; and the soul that sinneth, it shall die. The son
shall not be recompensed for the sins of his father, and the father shall not
be recompensed for the sins of his son; the righteousness of the righteous
f. 20 a 21 shall be upon him. If the wicked man turn from all his iniquity that he
hath done, and keep all My commandments, and do judgment and right-
22 eousness, he shall surely live, and shall not die, and all the iniquity that
he hath done shall not be remembered unto him, but in the righteousness

that he hath done shall he live; because I have no pleasure in the death of 23
the sinner, saith the Lord God, but every one that turneth from his evil
way shall live. And if the righteous turn away from his righteousness, 24
and do iniquity, according to all the iniquity that the wicked man hath
done, all his righteousness that he hath done shall not be remembered to
him, but in the iniquity that he hath done, in the sins that he hath sinned
shall he die. And ye say, His way is not good. Hear, ye house of Israel, 25
My way is good, but your ways are not good. If the righteous man 26
turn away from his righteousness, and do iniquity, in the iniquity that
he hath done shall he die; and if the wicked man turn away from his 27
iniquity that he hath done, and do judgment and righteousness, he shall
save his soul, because he hath turned from all his iniquity, he shall surely 28
live, and shall not die. And ye of the house of Israel say, The way of the 29
Lord is not good. My way is good, O ye of the house of Israel, but your
ways are not good. Because of this I will judge every one of you 30
according to his ways, saith the Lord God. Repent, and be converted
from all your iniquity and wickednesses, and these shall not be an evil
punishment to you. Cast away and remove from you all the wickedness 31
that ye have done wickedly, and make you a new heart and a new spirit,
and ye shall not die, O ye of the house of Israel. For I have no pleasure in 32
the death of the sinner, saith the Lord God, wherefore turn and live." See, Ap. Con. II. xv.
dear and beloved children, how many are the mercies of the Lord our God,
and His goodness and clemency towards us. He requireth from those who f. 20 b
have sinned that they repent; and in many places He speaketh about
these things, and giveth no place to the opinion of those who are hard-
hearted, and who wish to judge sharply and without mercy, and to cast
completely away those who have sinned, as if there were no repentance for
them. But God is not thus, but He calls even sinners to repentance, and
gives them hope, but those that have not sinned He teaches and says to
them, that they must not expect that we should bear or share in the sins
of others. Simply therefore receive those that repent, not doubting. For
He saith in the Prophet thus, "And thou, Son of man, say unto the children Ezek. xxxiii. 12
of thy people, The righteousness of the righteous shall not deliver him in
the day that he doeth evil, and the avarice of the wicked shall not hurt
him in the day that he repenteth from his iniquity; and the righteous
shall not be able to live in the day that he sinneth. When I say to 13
the righteous that he shall surely live, if he trust to his righteousness,
and do iniquity, all his righteousness that he hath done shall not be
remembered to him, but in the iniquity that he hath done shall he die.

14 When I say to the wicked that he shall surely die, and he turneth from
15 his sin, and doeth his righteousness; returneth the pledge which he hath
taken, and payeth back that which he hath violently robbed, and walketh
in the statutes and commandments of life that he may not do iniquity;
16 he shall surely live and not die, and all the sins that he hath sinned
shall not be remembered unto him; he hath done judgment and
17 righteousness, he shall surely live. And the children of thy people say,

(Cod. Sang. The way of the Lord God is not good. Say unto them, Your
18 ways are not good. If the righteous turn from his righteousness and do
19 iniquity, he shall surely die in his iniquity; and if the wicked turn from his
wickedness and do judgment and righteousness, he shall live thereby)."

It is required of you, O Bishops, according to the Scriptures, that ye judge those who sin with pity and mercy. For him that walketh on the brink of a river and falleth, if thou leave him in the river, thou pushest and throwest him down and committest murder; or when a man has fallen by
f. 21 a the side of a river's brink, and nearly perishes, stretch out thy hand to him quickly and draw him up that he perish not: thus therefore do, that thy people may learn and be wise, and also that he that sinneth, may not perish
Ap. Con. II. xvi. utterly, but that thou mayest look to him that hath sinned, be angry with him, and command them to put him out. And when he is put out[1], be ye not angry[1] with him, and contend with him, but let them keep him outside of the Church, and then let them go in and make supplication for him, for even our Saviour made supplication to His Father for those that had
Luke xxiii. 34 *sic* sinned, as it is written in the Gospel, "My Father, they know not what they do, nor what they speak, yet, if it be possible, forgive them." Then thou, O Bishop, command him to come in, and thyself ask him if he repents. If he be worthy to be received into the Church, appoint him days of fasting according to his fault, two, or three, or five, or seven weeks, and thus allow him to go, saying to him all that is proper for admonition and doctrine. Reprove him, and tell him to be humble-minded, and to pray and make supplication in the days of fasting, that he be found
Gen. iv. 7 worthy of the forgiveness of sins, as it is written in Genesis, "Thou hast sinned, cease. Let thy repentance be with thee, and thou shalt have power over it." Look also at Miriam the sister of Moses, when she had spoken against Moses, and afterwards she repented, and was thought
Numbers xii. 14 worthy of forgiveness, it was said by the Lord, "If her father had but spit in her face, would she not have been ashamed and separated for seven days without the camp, and then she would have come in?" Thus also

[1] S. let them be angry.

it is required of you to act towards those who promise to repent of their
sins. Put them out of the Church as it is proper for their faults, and
afterwards receive them as a merciful Father. If then the Bishop himself f. 21 b
cause scandal, how can he rise and search for the sin of any one, or Ap. Con. II. xvii.
reprove for it, and command sentence by his hands? by respect of persons
or gifts that they receive? either he or his deacons, whose conscience
is not clear. They cannot contend in the help of the Bishop, for they fear
lest they should hear as from a courageous man, this word that is
written in the Gospel, "Why seest thou the straw that is in thy brother's Matt. vii. 3
eye, but observest not the beam that is in thine own eye? Thou hypocrite, 5
take first the beam out of thine eye, and then shalt thou explore clearly to
take out the straw from thy brother's eye." Because [of this] therefore the
Bishop fears the Deacons, lest they hear the word of the Lord from him
that sinneth as from a courageous man. For he does not know that it
is dangerous for a man to speak against the Bishop, and in all that place
there will be a scandal, for he that hath sinned is wanting in reason, and
doth also not spare his soul. Because of this therefore for every reason for
which the Bishop fears, he makes himself as one who does not know him that
hath sinned, and he passes away from him, and does not reprove nor correct
him; and because of this, Satan, when he finds opportunity, will rule by
means of one, also of others. God forbid that this should be! and should
happen thus, that the flock becomes so as it can never again be[1], for many
sinners being found, evil becomes a force, because sinners are not corrected
and reproved so that they may repent. In every man there is an incitement
to sin, and it is fulfilled that was said, "My house shall be called a house of Is. lvi. 7
prayer for all peoples, but ye have made it a den of thieves." If then the Matt. xxi. 13
Bishop does not keep silence before them that sin, but reproves and censures f. 22 a
them, and corrects and admonishes and punishes him that hath sinned,
he also throws fear on others; for it is required of the Bishop that by
means of his doctrine he should be a preventer of sins unto death, and an
exhorter to righteousness, and by the admonition of his doctrine a guide
to good works, a glorifier and exalter of good things to come, that
are promised by God in the place of eternal life; and a preacher also
of future wrath by the judgment of God, by the threat of cruel fire,
quenchless and unbearable. Let him know the effect of the will of God,
that he may not despise any one, for our Saviour has said, "See that Matt.
ye despise not any one, not one of these little ones who believe in Me." xviii. 10
Therefore let the Bishop care for every one: for those who have not sinned Ap. Con. II. xviii.

[1] S. + established.

that they may remain as they are without sin; also for those who have sinned, that they may repent, and let him give them pardon for their sins,
Is. lviii. 6 as it is written in Isaiah that the Lord hath said, "Loose all the bands of wickedness, and cut all the burdens of deceit and of oppression."

[CHAPTER VII. in Cod. S.]

Therefore, O Bishop, teach, and reprove, and loosen by pardon, and know that thy place is that of God Almighty, and thou hast received
Matt. xviii. 18 power to forgive sins, for it is said to you Bishops, "All that ye shall bind on earth shall be bound in Heaven; and all that ye shall loose shall be loosed." As therefore thou hast power to loose, know thyself and thy conduct and thy works, that in this life they may be (S. worthy) of thy place, but there is no man among the sons of men who is without
Job xiv. 4 sins, for it is written, "There is no man that is pure from the uncleanness of sin, no, not one, even if he have lived only one day in this world." Because of this the conversation and the conduct of the works of the righteous, and of the first Fathers were written, that it might be known
f. 22 b that in each one of them was found just a little sin, that it might be
Psalm li. 4 known that the Lord God alone is sinless, as David said, "That thou mightest be justified in thy sayings and be clear in thy judgments." For the uncleanness of the righteous is to ourselves a comfort and a consolation and a good hope, that we, though we have also sinned a little, have an expectation of getting pardon. There is therefore no man without sin. But thou, according to thy strength, be diligent that thou be not overtaken in aught, and be careful about every one, lest any man should be offended, and should perish because of thee; because the layman is careful of his own soul alone, but thou carriest the weight of every man, and it is a very
Luke xii. 48 great burden that thou bearest; "for he to whom the Lord hath given much, from him much will be required." Forasmuch, therefore, as thou bearest the burdens of all men, be watchful. For it is written that the
Numbers xviii. 1 *sic* Lord said to Moses, "Thou and Aaron shall bear the sins of the priesthood." For thus, as thou shalt give a sufficient answer for many, so thou shalt care for every one; that thou mayest keep those that are whole, and admonish those that sin, and correct and reprove and punish and lighten them by means of repentance and pardon; and when a sinner repents and weeps, receive him; and when the people have prayed for him, lay [thy hands] upon him, and allow him thenceforth to be in the Church. Those who sleep and are negligent restore and rouse and confirm, and pray for them and heal them, for thou knowest where is the reward to thee if

thou hast done thus; so if thou neglectest it, a great danger will come upon
thee. For the Lord hath said in Ezekiel about the Bishops who despise
their people thus: "The word of the Lord came unto me, saying, Son **Ezekiel**
of man, prophesy against the shepherds of Israel, and say unto them, **xxxiv. 1, 2**
Thus saith the Lord God, Woe to the shepherds of Israel that do feed
themselves, and the shepherds do not feed My flock. Ye eat the milk, **3** f. 23 a
and clothe yourselves with the wool, and ye kill her that is fat, but ye
feed not the flocks. Her that is sick have ye not cured; her that **4**
is weak have ye not strengthened; her that was broken have ye
not bound up; her that had wandered have ye not brought back;
and her that was lost have ye not found; but with violence and
levity have ye ruled them; and My flock is scattered without a **5**
shepherd; it has become meat to the beasts of the field. My own flocks **6**
are wandering on all high mountains and on all the face of the earth." **Matt.**
Thou shalt leave the ninety and nine on the mountain, and go to seek **xviii. 12 Ap. Con.**
her that was lost; and when thou findest her carry her upon thy **II. xx b.**
shoulders, rejoicing, because thou hast found her that was lost; bring
her and mingle her with the flock. Thus obey thou also, O Bishop;
visit the one that is lost, and seek the one that has wandered, and
restore the one that is far away, because thou hast power to forgive
the sins of him that has fallen...for thou fillest the place of the Christ.
Because of this also our Saviour said to him that had sinned, "Thy sins **Matt. ix. 2**
are forgiven thee; thy faith hath made thee whole; go in peace." Peace *sic*
then is the Church of quiet and rest; she in whom He established
those whom He loosed from their sins whole and without spot, having
a good hope, and being diligent in the cultivation of works and
afflictions. As a wise and sympathetic physician He cures all men,
and mostly those who have wandered in their sins, for "the whole have **Mark ii. 17**
no need of a physician, but they that are sick." Thou also, O Bishop, art
made the physician of His Church, therefore do not restrain the medicine
that thou mayest heal those that are sick in their sins, but cure them by
every means and make them whole and establish them safe in the Church; f. 23 b
that thou be not taken by this word which the Lord spake, "Ye have **Ezekiel xxxiv. 4**
ruled them with violence and levity." Lead not therefore with violence; **Ap. Con.**
be not vehement, nor judge sharply, nor be merciless, nor deride the **II. xxi.**
people who are under thy hand, nor hide from them the word of
repentance, for that would be to have ruled them with violence and
levity. But if ye oversee my people harshly and punish them with
violence, and drive them and expel them, and do not receive them that

have sinned, but harshly and mercilessly hide repentance from them,
thou wilt even be a helper in their conversion to evil, and in scattering
the flocks to be food for the beasts of the field, that is to say, to the
wicked men of this world, but not to men in truth, but to the beasts,
to the heathen, to the heretics; for him who goes out of the Church they
follow immediately, like evil beasts, to swallow him for food; because
of thine own harshness, he then that goeth out of the Church, either goeth
and entereth in unto the heathen, or plunges into heresies; he will be
entirely a stranger, and be removed from the Church, and from the hope
of God, and thou wilt be guilty of his ruin, because thou wert ready to
put out and to cast away those who sin; and when they repented and
returned, thou didst not wish to receive them. Behold, thou art fallen
Romans iii. 15 under the condemnation of this word which said, "Your feet hasten to
iii. 16 evil, and are swift to shed blood; affliction and misery are in their
paths, and the way of peace have they not known." The Way of Peace
Luke vi. 37 is our Saviour, as He said, "Forgive the sins of those who sin, that
your sins also may be forgiven; give and it shall be given unto you,"
f. 24 a which is, "Give the pardon of sins, that you also may receive pardon."
He also teaches us that we should be constant in prayers at all times,
Matt. vi. 12 and that we should say, "Forgive us our debts and our sins, as we also
forgive our debtors." For if thou forgivest not those that sin, how canst
thou receive forgiveness? Behold, will not thy mouth accuse thee, and
thou wilt convict thyself of having said, "I forgive" when thou hast
not forgiven, but hast verily murdered; for he who puts any one out
of the Church without mercy, what else does he do but murder bitterly,
and shed blood without pity? For if a righteous man is unjustly killed
by any one by means of the sword, he is received to rest with God;
but he who puts any one out of the Church and receives him not again,
kills verily evilly and bitterly for eternity; and God gives to be food
to cruel fire for ever, him who puts out of the Church, and does not
look at the mercy of God, and does not remember His goodness to
the penitent, and does not bear the likeness of the Christ, nor pay
attention to any people who repent of the multitude of their failings that
Ap. Con. II. xxii. they may receive pardon from him. It is required of thee then, O Bishop,
that the things which happened of old should be put before thine eyes,
that from them thou mayest understand and be taught the cure of
souls, and admonition and reproof and intercession. When thou judgest
men, compare cautiously and with much investigation, and cleave to
the will of God; and according as He acts, thus ought ye also to act

in your judgments. Hear therefore, O Bishop, in regard to these things,
an example that is congruous and helpful. It is written in the fourth
Book of Kingdoms, and in the second Book of Days thus, that "in these f. 24 b
days Manasseh reigned, being twelve years old, and for fifty years he 2 Kings xxi. 1
reigned in Jerusalem; the name of his mother was Apheeba (Hephzi-bah). 2 Chron. xxxiii. 1
He did that which was evil before the Lord, like the abomination of 2
the peoples, whom the Lord had destroyed before the children of Israel."
He returned and built the high places for the sacrifices which Hezekiah 3
his father had thrown down. He raised statues to Baal, and made
abominations like as Ahab king of Israel had done. He made altars
to all the army of Heaven, and worshipped all the powers of Heaven.
He built an altar to demons in the house of the Lord, where the Lord 4
had said, "In Jerusalem is My house, I will put My name there for ever."
Manasseh served the high places and said, My name shall endure for ever.
He built an altar to all the army of Heaven in the two courts of the
house of the Lord. "He caused his children to pass through the fire 2 Chron. xxxiii. 6
in the valley of the son of Hinnom; he used auguries and sorceries;
he made soothsayings and incantations and divinations, and wrought
many evil things in the eyes of the Lord, to provoke Him to anger.
He set a molten and carved image of the abomination which he had 7
made, in the house of the Lord, where the Lord had said to David and to
Solomon his son, that in this house, and in Jerusalem which I have chosen
from all the tribes of Israel, I will put My name for ever. Nor will I 8
any more restrain My feet from the land of Israel which I have given
to your fathers, only if they keep all that I have commanded them,
according to all the commandments which I commanded my servant
Moses, and they did not hear. Manasseh caused them to err, to do 9
evil before the Lord, according to the works of the nations whom the 2 Kings xxi. 10
Lord had destroyed before the children of Israel." "The Lord spake with f. 25 a
Manasseh, and to his people by the hand of his servants the prophets,
and said, Because Manasseh king of Judah has done these abominations 11
in Jerusalem, like as did the Amorites who were before him, and has
also made Judah to sin by his idols; therefore thus saith the Lord God 12
of Israel, Behold I bring such evil things upon Jerusalem and upon Judah,
that the two ears of every one that heareth them shall tingle. I will 13
stretch over Jerusalem that measure of Samaria, and the weight of
the house of Ahab, and I will wipe Jerusalem as one wipeth a water-
vessel when he turneth it on its face. I will give the remnant of Mine 14
inheritance to the sword, and will deliver them into the hand of their

enemies, and they shall be for a prey and a spoil to all that hate them, because they have done evil before mine eyes, because they have been provoking from that day that I have brought out their fathers from Egypt until this day. Manasseh also shed much innocent blood, till he had filled Jerusalem from rim to rim with the slain, because of the sins which he com-
2 Chron. xxxiii. 11 mitted; and he made Judah to sin in doing evil before the Lord." "And He brought against them the captains of Assyria; and they took Manasseh and bound him, and threw chains about him and carried him to Babylon in a copper star, and shut him up in prison, having completely chained and bound him in irons." Bread of husks was given to him by weight, and water mixed with vinegar in small measure, that he might
2 Chron. xxxiii. 12 be alive and afflicted and heavily troubled. "When he was much afflicted he sought the face of the Lord his God, and humbled himself greatly before the God of his fathers." He prayed to the Lord God, and said:

f. 25 b *The Prayer of Manasseh.*

Lord God of my fathers! God of Abraham and Isaac and Jacob, and of their righteous seed, who hast made the heavens with all their array, who hast chained the sea and established it by the command of Thy word, who hast bound the abyss and hast sealed it by Thine awful and glorious name; Thou before whose power everything trembles and shakes because of the unbearable greatness of the splendour of Thy glory, and no man can bear to stand before the anger of Thy wrath against sinners; whose mercies are infinite and measureless; for Thou art a Lord who is longsuffering and merciful and very gracious, and Thou regrettest the evils of the sons of man; Thou, Lord, according to the kindness of Thy goodness, hast promised forgiveness to those who repent of their sins, and in the greatness of Thy mercies Thou hast appointed repentance for the salvation of sinners. Thou, therefore, Lord God of the righteous, didst not appoint repentance to our father Abraham, and Isaac and Jacob, nor even to those who had never sinned against Thee. Yet thou hast appointed repentance to me, for I am a sinner, because my sins are more than the sand of the sea. I have not breath to lift up my head for the multitude of my iniquities. And now, Lord God[1], behold, I am justly afflicted, and I am grieved as I deserve. Behold, I am chained and bent by a multitude of iron chains, so that I cannot lift up my head. Nor am I worthy to lift up mine eyes and look and see the height of heaven because of the multitude of my wickednesses, for I have done evil things before Thee, and I have kindled Thy wrath and set up idols, and multiplied

[1] S. om. God.

abominations. And now behold, I bend the knees of my heart before Thee, and seek Thy kindness. I have sinned, Lord, I have sinned. Because I know my sins, I supplicate before Thee, forgive me, Lord, and destroy me not in my follies. Be not angry with me for ever, nor keep my evil f. 26 a
deeds, nor hold me guilty nor cast me down to the lower parts of the earth. For Thou, O Lord, art the God of those who repent, therefore even in me, Lord, shew Thy goodness, for though I am unworthy, save me according to Thy mercies. Therefore I will praise Thee at all times, and all the days of my life; for all the powers of Heaven praise Thee, and sing to Thee for ever and ever. And the Lord heard the voice of Manasseh, and had mercy upon him. There came upon him a flame of fire, and all the irons with which he was chained were melted and loosened; and the Lord delivered Manasseh from his afflictions, and restored him to Jerusalem to his kingdom; and Manasseh knew the Lord, and said that He was God alone, with all his heart and with all his soul all the days of his life. He was counted righteous, and slept with his fathers, and Amon his son reigned after him. Ye have heard, dear children. Like as Manasseh worshipped evil idols bitterly, and killed the righteous, and when he repented, the Lord forgave him, although there is no sin worse than the worship of idols, yet a place Ap. Con.
for repentance was given. But to him who saith, Good things shall happen II. xxiii.
to me though I walk in the perverse will of my heart, thus saith the Lord, I will stretch out My hand upon him, and he shall be for a history and a proverb, because Amon son of Manasseh having taken counsel with the counsel of law-breaking said, My father from his childhood was very wicked, and good in his old age; I also will act now according to the lusts of my soul, and at the last I will repent towards the Lord. He did that which is evil before the Lord. He reigned two years only. Therefore the Lord God destroyed him from the good land. Therefore take heed, Ap. Con. II. xxiv.
ye who have no faith, lest any of you should confirm in his heart the f. 26 b
calculation of Amon son of Manasseh and perish quickly and swiftly. Therefore, O Bishop, keep with strength as thou canst those who have not sinned, that they may remain without sinning, and those who repent of sins heal and receive. For if thou receive not him who repents, because thou art merciless, thou sinnest against the Lord God, because thou dost not obey our Lord and God in acting as He acted; for even He to that woman who had sinned, her whom the elders placed before him and left it to judgment at His hands, and went away; He then who searcheth the hearts, asked her and said to her, "Have the Elders condemned thee, my John viii. 11
daughter? She saith to him, No, Lord. And our Saviour said, Go, and

return no more to do this, neither do I condemn thee." In this therefore let our Saviour and King and God be to you a sign, O Bishops! be like Him, that ye may be gentle and humble and merciful and clement, and peacemakers and without anger, teachers, and reprovers, and receivers and persuaders. Be not wrathful and be not tyrants, nor contemptuous, nor haughty, nor boasters.

CHAPTER VII.

Again a broad doctrine about the Bishop himself, that with much diligence he take care of his flock and admonish and encourage them, and teach them, that they may not cut off hope about themselves when they fall; and a great consolation to those who are shaken and are converted repenting, and a great condemnation upon the Bishop who receiveth not those who repent, and a command to him that he be gentle and kind towards the children of his people,
Ap. Con. II. xviii b. *and be not harsh and angry.*

Ezekiel xxxiv. 7 "Therefore, ye shepherds, hear the word of the Lord God. Forasmuch
8 as my flock is for a prey and for meat to all the beasts of the wilderness,
without a shepherd, and the shepherds have not sought my flock, but the
f. 27 a 9 shepherds fed themselves, and fed not my flock, therefore, ye shepherds,
10 hear the word of the Lord. Thus saith the Lord God, Behold, I am
against the shepherds, and I will require My flock at your hands, and
cause them to cease from any more feeding My flock; neither shall the
shepherds feed themselves any more, but I will deliver My flock from your
11 hands, that they may not be meat for them. For thus saith the Lord God,
12 Therefore behold I will visit my flock, and will seek them out, as a
shepherd seeketh out his flock in the day of storm, being amongst them,
thus will I seek out my flock and gather it, from all the places where they
13 have been scattered, in the day of cloud and darkness. And I will bring
them out from the peoples, and gather them from the lands, and bring
them into their own land, and I will feed them upon the mountains of
14 Israel, and in all the waste places of the land. In a good and fat pasture
I will feed them, and upon the high mountains of Israel shall be the glory
of their splendour, and there they shall lie in a good fold, and in a fat
15 pasture shall they feed in the mountains of Israel. I will feed My flock,
16 and I will establish[1] them, saith the Lord God, I will seek that which is
lost, and restore that which has wandered, and bind up that which is broken,
and strengthen that which is sick, and I will keep that which is fat and
17 strong, and will feed them with judgment. And you My flock, the flocks

[1] S. send.

of My pasture, thus saith the Lord my Lord, Behold I judge between sheep
and sheep, and between ram and ram. Is it a small thing unto you 18
that ye eat up the good and fat pasture, and the rest of your pasture
ye tread down with your feet, and My flock drank what is trodden 19
down by your feet. Therefore thus saith the Lord my Lord, Behold I judge 20
between sheep and sheep, and between those that are sick; because ye 21
thrust with your sides and your shoulders, and with your horns ye pierced
all the sick ones, until ye scattered them out. And I will save My flock, 22
and they shall no more be for a prey; and I will judge between sheep and
sheep. And I will set up [1]a shepherd over them[1], and David My servant 23 f. 27 b
shall be captain among them, I the Lord have spoken. I will make with 25
them a covenant of peace, and will cause the evil beasts to cease out of the
land, and they shall dwell safely in the wilderness, and sleep in the wood;
and I will give them a blessing round about my hills. I will send down 26
the rain in its season and it shall be a rain of blessings. The trees of the 27
field shall yield their fruit, and the earth shall yield her produce, and they
shall dwell safely in their land; and they shall know that I am the Lord,
when I have cut the nooses of their yoke, and I have delivered them from
the hand of those who made them to serve. And they shall no more be for 28
a prey, nor shall the beast of the field devour them; but they shall dwell
safely, and there shall be none to make them afraid. And I will raise up 29
for them a Plant of renown[2], that they may no more bear the shame of the
nations; and they shall know that I the Lord their God am with them, 30
and that they of the house of Israel are My people, saith the Lord God."

Hear therefore, ye Bishops, and hear, ye laymen, that as the Lord hath said, I will judge between ram and ram, and between sheep and sheep, that is to say, between Bishop and Bishop, and between layman and layman; for if the layman love the layman, let the layman also love the Bishop and honour him, and reverence him as father and lord and god after God Almighty, for it is said to the Bishop by means of the Apostles, that "all who hear you hear Me, and all that injure you injure Me, and Him that sent Me." Again, let the Bishop love the laymen as children, and nourish and inflame[3] them with the zeal of his love, like eggs, that chickens may come from them; hatch them like chickens and nourish them as with the nourishment of winged fowls. O Bishop! teach and admonish every one. Those who are deserving of reproof reprove, and make them sorry, as for conversion and not for destruction. Admonish as for repentance, and

Ap. Con. II. xix. **Ap. Con. II. xx.** **Luke x. 16** *sic* f. 28 a

[1] S. one Shepherd over them, and he shall feed them, and he shall be their shepherd.
[2] S. peace + that they may no more be few and abandoned upon the earth, and
[3] Cod. admonish.

correct them, so that thou mayest make their ways straight and smooth for them, and make stable their mode of life. Keep what is in health, that is to say, keep carefully him who is steadfast in the faith, and feed all the people in peace. That which is weak strengthen, that is to say, him who is tempted, strengthen by means of admonition. That which is sick heal, that is to say, him who is sick with doubt of the faith heal by means of doctrine. That which is broken bind up, that is to say, him who is beaten or struck or broken by his sins or halting in the way of righteousness, bind him up, that is to say, cure him by means of intercession and admonition; raise him from his fall and encourage him; shew him also that there is hope for him. Bind him up and heal him; admit him also to the Church. That which has wandered persuade, that is to say, him that is abandoned in sins, and excommunicated as for reproof, leave not without, but teach and admonish and convert, and receive him into thy flock, that is to say, him who by the multitude of his falls has cut off his hope, and has let his soul go to perdition; do not allow him to perish utterly, lest by means of temptation or much negligence he sleep, and through the heaviness of his slumber he forget his life, and be removed and turned from the flock, that is to say, from the Church, and he come to perdition; for since he has got out of the fold and is removed from the flock, a wolf will eat him as he wanders, and he will perish utterly. But
f. 28 b do thou visit him, admonish and teach and convert him, command him and encourage him to awaken; tell him that there is hope, and cut this off from their minds, that they may not say nor think that which was
Ezekiel xxxiii. 10 said of old, that "Our iniquities and sins are upon us, and by them we are corrupted; how then can we live?" It is not required of us that we should say or think these things, or suppose that their hope is cut off on account of the multitude of their sins, but that they should know that the mercies of God are many, that He hath promised with oaths and good counsel, pardon to those who have sinned. If then a man sin, and know not the Scriptures, and be not persuaded of the long-suffering and pity of God, and knoweth not the boundaries of pardon and repentance, he perisheth by this, that he knoweth not. Therefore thou, O Bishop, as a shepherd, a partaker in suffering, who art full of love and tenderness, be assiduous in visiting thy flock. Count the flock. Seek that which has wandered, as said the Lord God Jesus the Christ, our Teacher and our Good Shepherd.

CHAPTER VIII.

Teaches the same Bishop that he be not luxurious and covetous about the things that come into the Church, as provision for the poor, but that he furnish them with justice to those that are in want, as a just steward of God, and that he also may supply his own want out of them without guilt; and that he also stir up the people, that every one according to his ability take a share, and supply the need of the Church, in regard to the provision for the poor and for orphans and widows.

Be not lovers of wine, nor drunkards, nor much puffed up, nor luxurious. Do not incur expense that is not proper from the gifts of God, as if it were not your own, but as if you were making use of your own; as those who are appointed to be good stewards of God, of Him who will in future require at your hands an account of the management of the stewardship with which you are entrusted. Let your sufficiency then be enough for you, food and raiment; make use of what is necessary and not beyond what is just from the things that come in, as from strange things, but in moderation; do not enjoy yourselves and be luxurious from the income of the Church, for to a workman his raiment and food are sufficient. Therefore as good stewards of God, do well in dispensing the things that are given and come into the Church, according to the commandment, to the orphans and widows and those who are in straits and to strangers, like men who know that ye have a God who requires at your hands an account of the stewardship which He has committed to you. Therefore distribute and give to every one who is in want, also yourselves provide and live from these things, from the things that come into the Church. Do not consume them yourselves alone, but give a share with yourselves to those who are in want. Be without offence before God; because God reproves Bishops who use the income of the Church avariciously and for themselves alone, and do not give a share with them to the poor. The Lord said thus, "Ye eat the milk of the flocks, and ye clothe yourselves with the wool." For it is required of you Bishops that ye be provided for out of the income of the Church, but not that ye swallow it up; for it is written, "Thou shalt not muzzle the ox that grinds." Thus therefore as the ox that works in the threshing-floor without a muzzle eats food, but does not consume it all, thus also ye who labour in the threshing-floor, which is the Church of God, provide for yourselves from the Church, like the Levites who served in the Tabernacle of witness, which was the type of the Church, as its very name tells, for the Tabernacle of witness set forth the Church beforehand. Therefore the Levites who served in it were provided for without hindrance from the things that were given as the offerings of God by all the people, gifts, and oblations and first-fruits and tithes and sacrifices, and offerings and whole burnt-offerings,

Ap. Con. II. xxiv b. xxv.

f. 29 a

Ezekiel xxxiv. 3

Deut. xxv. 4

f. 29 b

they and their wives and their sons and daughters, because their work was the service of the Tabernacle alone. Therefore they received no inheritance of land among the children of Israel, for the inheritance of Levi and of his tribe was the inheritance[1] of the people. Therefore ye also to-day, O Bishops, are priests to your people, and Levites who serve in the house of God, the Holy Catholic Church, those who remain continually before the Lord God. Therefore ye are to your people priests and prophets and chiefs and governors and teachers and mediators between God and the believers, receivers of the Word, preachers of it, evangelists of it, knowers of the Scriptures and of the words of God, witnesses of His will, ye who bear the sins of all men, and who will give account concerning all men; ye who hear how that word is kindled hardly against you, if ye despise, and do not preach the will of God, ye are they who are in grave danger of perdition, if ye despise your people. Ye again are those to whom is promised by God a great reward that will not disappoint nor be snatched away, and unspeakable grace in that great glory, if ye serve well the Tabernacle of God, the Catholic Church. Therefore as ye bear the burden of all men, thus also it is required of you that ye receive from all who are
f. 30 a with you the service of food and clothing, and other things, such as are necessary. It is required also that ye take from the gifts that are given you by the people who are under your hands, and provide for the deacons and the widows and the orphans, and those that are in want. For it is required of thee, Bishop, that thou care for all men as a faithful steward, for as thou carriest the weight of all those who are under thy hands, thus, and more than all men, thou shalt receive the glory of excellency from God; for thou art the propitiator[2] of the Christ; and as He has borne the sins of us all, thus it is required of thee that thou carry the sins of all those who are under thy hands. For thus it is written in
Is. liii. 2 Isaiah about our Saviour, "We have seen Him, that He had no splendour
lii. 14 and no beauty, but His visage was more shamed and humiliated than
liii. 3 men, and that He was a man of suffering; and knoweth [3][how] to under-
4 stand[3] sicknesses; for His face was changed and done despite to, and
He was of no account in our eyes. He then hath carried our sins,
and for us He died; and we thought Him wounded and grieved and
5 humiliated. But He was wounded for our sins, and afflicted for our
iniquities, and by His wounds we are all healed." Again he saith, that
12 "He bore the sins of many, and was betrayed because of their iniquity."

[1] S. offerings [2] S. imitator [3] S. to bear

And in David and in all the Prophets and also in the Gospel, our Saviour
entreats on account of our sins, He who was without sins. Therefore
as ye have the example of the Christ, thus also be ye an example to the
people that are under your hands, that as He hath taken our sins (S. so
do ye also take the sins of the people). Do not imagine that the burden
of the Bishopric is a light and easy one. Therefore as ye have received
the burden of all men, thus also the fruits which ye draw from all the
people, are yours for all things that are necessary to you. Provide well f. 30 b
for those that are in want, like people who give account to an inquisitor
who does not err and cannot be got over. As ye serve in the office of
the bishopric, thus it is meet that from the office of the bishopric
ye provide for yourselves; like priests and Levites and deacons who
serve before God; as it is written in the Book of Numbers, that
God spake to Aaron and said, "Thou, and thy sons, and thy father's Numbers xviii. 1
house shall bear the sins of the holy things; and thou and thy sons
shall bear the sins of the priesthood; and thy brethren the sons of thy 2
father, the tribe of Levi, bring with thee; let them be placed beside thee
and let them serve thee. Thou and thy sons with thee shall serve before
this Tabernacle of witness, except that the sons of Levi shall not approach 3
the vessels of the sanctuary nor the altar, that they and ye die not;
but they shall be added unto thee, and they shall keep the watches of 4
the Tabernacle of witness for all the service of the Tabernacle, and a
stranger shall not come nigh unto thee. Ye shall keep these charges 5
of the holy things, and the charges of the altar; and there shall be no
wrath upon the children of Israel. And behold, I have taken your 6
brethren the sons of Levi from among the children of Israel, they are
given as a gift to the Lord, to do the service of the Tabernacle of witness.
Thou, and thy sons with thee, keep your priesthood for all the service 7
of the altar, and of that within the Veil; do your service, as something
that is given to your Priesthood; the stranger that cometh nigh shall
die the death. And the Lord spake unto Moses and unto Aaron, and 8
said, Behold, I have given you the charges and the firstfruits of all
that is hallowed to me by the children of Israel, to thee I have given
them for service, and to thy sons after thee, a law for ever. This shall 9
be thine of all the holy things that are hallowed from their fruits and f. 31 a
from their offerings, and from all their sacrifices, from all their errors
and from all their sins, all that they offer to Me of all the holy things,
let it be for thee and for thy sons; eat it in the Holy place; every male 10
shall eat it, thou and thy sons, it shall be holy to thee. These shall be 11

to you, the firstfruits of their gifts, from all the oblations of the children
of Israel, to thee I have given them, and to thy sons and thy daughters
with thee, for an everlasting law; every one that is clean in thy house
12 shall eat them, all the firstfruits of the oil, and all the firstfruits of the
wine, and the firstfruits of the wheat, all that they give to the Lord
shall be thine; every one that is clean in thy house shall eat of them.
13, 15 All [1]the rest that remains[1] shall be thine, and all that openeth the matrix
of all flesh, all that they bring to the Lord, of men and even of beasts
shall be thine; nevertheless the firstborn of men shall surely be redeemed,
16 and the firstborn of beasts that are not clean to be offered; and their
redemption shall be from a month old and upwards; thou shalt redeem
them for a price, five shekels by the shekel of the sanctuary, which is
17 ten[2] shekels of silver. But nevertheless the firstlings of oxen, and the
firstlings of sheep and goats, thou shalt not redeem; they are holy;
thou shalt pour out their blood before the altar, and their fat thou shalt
18 send up as an offering of a sweet savour unto the Lord; and their flesh
shall be pure to thee, the end of the wave breast and the right forefoot
19 shall be thine. All the heave offerings of the sanctuary, which the
children of Israel destine to the Lord, to thee have I given them, to thy
sons and also to thy daughters with thee, for an everlasting law: it shall
be a statute for ever before the Lord, to thee and to thy seed after thee.
f. 31 b 20 And the Lord spake unto Aaron, and said, Thou shalt not inherit in
their land, nor have any portion among them, because I am thy portion
21 and thine inheritance among the children of Israel. And behold, to the
children of Levi I have given all the tithes of the children of Israel
22 for an inheritance, on account of their service in the Tabernacle. And
the children of Israel shall not again come nigh unto the Tabernacle
23 of witness, that they receive not the sin of death, but the Levites
shall do the service of the Tabernacle of witness, and they shall bear
their sins, as an everlasting law to their generations. And among the
24 children of Israel they shall have no inheritance, because that the
tithes of the children of Israel which they destine as heave offerings
to the Lord, I have given to the Levites as an inheritance; therefore
I said unto them, and to those of the house of Israel, that they shall
25 have no inheritance for ever. The Lord spake unto Moses and said to
26 him, Speak with the Levites, and say unto them, When ye take from
the children of Israel the tithes that I have given you from them as an

[1] S. that is dedicated by the children of Israel

[2] S. twenty

inheritance, offer up from them also an heave offering to the Lord, even
a tenth part of the tithes. The heave offering shall be reckoned to you 27
as the wheat of the threshing-floor, and as the offering of the wine-press.
Thus ye also shall offer a heave offering unto the Lord of all your tithes 28
which ye receive from all the children of Israel, and ye shall give of
them a heave offering to the Lord, to Aaron the priest, of all your gifts 29
ye shall offer a heave offering to the Lord, of the firstfruits which He hath
sanctified. And say unto them, When ye offer the firstfruits of them, 30
it shall be reckoned unto the Levites as the produce of the threshing-floor,
and as the produce of the wine-press; they shall eat it in every place, 31
ye and your households, because that is your reward for your service
in the Tabernacle of witness, and ye shall have no sin because of it, f. 32 a 32
when ye have offered the firstfruits of it; ye shall not pollute the offerings
of the children of Israel, that ye die not."

CHAPTER IX.

Exhortation to the people that they bring heave offerings of prayers and confessions to God, and that they honour the Bishop as [they honour] God, and reverence him, and that they do nothing apart from his permission, nor even give alms to those that are in need without him; but make everything known to him by means of the Deacon, and he will administer whatever is given, and that every one of the orders of the Church take its place and be honoured as befits it; condemnation and commination on those who speak wickedly to priests or despise them; that they think of them as of their kings, that they take them gifts from their labour for the supply of the need of the poor and the orphans and the widows, making no reckoning with them, as to whether they give or do not give.

Hear, therefore, these things, ye also, ye laymen, the Church chosen of God, because that even the first people was called the Church. Ye then, Holy and perfect Catholic Church, royal priesthood, holy assembly, people of inheritance, great Church, Bride adorned for the Lord God. As therefore was said before, hear also now, Bring heave offerings and tithes and firstfruits to the Christ, the true High Priest, also to His servants bring tithes of salvation, Him the beginning of whose name is the letter 10. Hear, thou Catholic Church, which art of God, who hast been delivered from 10 plagues, and hast received 10 commandments, and hast learnt the law and hast held the faith, and hast believed in a *yod* the beginning of a name, and art confirmed by the perfection of His glory; instead of the sacrifices of that time, offer now prayers and supplications and thanks-

f. 32 b givings; then were firstfruits and tithes and oblations and gifts, to-day are offerings that are presented by means of the Bishops to the Lord God, for those are your High Priests. Priests and Levites; now Elders and Deacons, and Orphans and Widows. For the Levite and the High Priest is the Bishop. He is a servant of the Word of God and a Mediator, but to you a Teacher and your Father after God, who has begotten you by means of water. He is your Head and Governor, and he is a powerful king to you. He governs in the place of the Almighty, but let him be honoured by you as God, because the Bishop sits for you in the place of Almighty God; but the Deacon stands in the place of the Christ; and ye should love him, but let the Deaconesses be honoured by you in the likeness of the Holy Ghost. Moreover, let the Elders be to you in the likeness of the Apostles, but Orphans and Widows be considered by you in the likeness of an Altar. For as it was not allowed for the stranger, that is to say for him who was not a Levite, to approach the Altar, nor to offer anything apart from the High Priest, thus do ye naught apart from the Bishop. For if any one do aught apart from the Bishop, he doeth it in vain, for it will not be counted to him as a work, because it is not fitting that any one should do aught without the High Priest. Present, therefore, your offerings to the Bishop, either ye yourselves, or by means of the Deacons; and what he receives let him deal to you justly, for the Bishop is well acquainted with those who are afflicted; for he provides for every one and gives as it becomes him; lest any one should receive many times in the day or in the week, and another should not receive even a little. For to him whom the priest and steward of God knows to be much afflicted, he does good, as is required of him. And those who ask widows to *agapai*, her whom he knows to be much afflicted, to her let him send oftenest. And again, if any one give gifts to widows, to her who is in want let him send most. Let the portion of a shepherd be defined and known, [1]according as the law of old is defined[1], and even if he be not present [2]ye shall not cause to perish [any that belong] to[2] God Almighty. As often then as is given to you or[3] the widows, let double be given to each of the Deacons for the honour of the Christ; twice double to the Governor for the honour of God Almighty. If any man wish also to honour the Elders, let him give also (S. + double) to them as to the Deacons. For it is required for them that they be honoured as Apostles, and as the counsellors of the Bishop, and also as the crown of the Church; for they are the directors and counsellors of the

Ap. Con. II. xxvi. — Ap. Con. II. xxvii. — f. 33 a — Ap. Con. II. xxviii.

[1] according to the law in *agapai* and gifts
[2] to the honour of
[3] S. + to each of

Church. And if there be also a Reader, let him also receive along with the Elders. Every office, therefore, let each of the laity as is proper to him, honour by gifts, by dignity, and the respect of the world. Let them have great boldness with the Deacons, and let them not be troubling the Chief at all hours, but whatever they require, let them make it known by means of the servants, that is to say, by means of the Deacons. For not even to God Almighty can one approach save by means of the Christ. All things, therefore, that ye wish to have done, make them known to the Bishop by means of the Deacons, and then let them be done. Not even of old in the Temple of the Sanctuary was anything offered or done apart from the Priest. Again also, with the idols of the heathen, polluted and abominable and reprehensible, even to our day they imitate the Sanctuary, f. 33 b
though in comparison the house of impurity is very far from the Holy place; but nevertheless in the work of their oversight (in another manuscript, of their folly), without their polluted priests they do not offer nor do anything; but thus they suppose that the mouth of the stones (that is to say, the idols he calls stones) is a polluted priest, and they wait for whatever he commands them to do, and in all that they contemplate doing they are counselled by their polluted priest, and they do nothing without him, for they think that this is acceptable whatever they do, honouring him and doing homage to him like their honouring of the dumb stones, those that are fixed as stones (S. in the walls) for the worship of impure and cruel demons. If they, therefore, who are foolish and [have] false customs and no hope, but err by a vain expectation, watch and desire to imitate a sanctuary, and honour with every honour those who stand in the house of their ridiculous idols, why then ye to whom it is known and manifest that ye believe in the truth, and are possessed by a hope that will not be falsified, and look to the promise of eternal glory which passeth not away nor dissolveth, should not ye the more honour the Lord God, by means of those who are appointed over you? Consider, therefore, the Bishop as the mouth of God. **Ap. Con. II. xxix.**
For if Aaron, because he interpreted to Pharaoh the words that were given through Moses, was called a Prophet, as the Lord said unto Moses, "Behold, I have given thee for a god unto Pharaoh, and Aaron thy **Ex. vii. 1**
brother shall be thy prophet," why, therefore, do ye also not consider (S. + as prophets, and adore) as God those who are to you mediators of the Word? Now for us ourselves, Aaron is the Deacon, and Moses **Ap. Con. II. xxx.**
the Bishop[1]. Let him be honoured by you as God, and the Deacon as f. 34 a

[1] S. + for if Moses was called a god by the Lord, let the Bishop be also by you.

Ap. Con. II. xxxi. a Prophet. Therefore for the honour of the Bishop make known to him
everything that ye do. Even by means of him let everything be com-
xxxii. pleted. If ye know that a man is much afflicted, but the Bishop
doth not know it, inform him, but without him do nothing to disgrace
him that thou bring no shame upon him as upon a despiser of
the poor; for he who raises an evil report against the Bishop either
by word or by deed, sins against God Almighty. But again, against
a Deacon if any one speak evilly by word or by deed, he offends the
Ex. xxii. 28 Christ. Therefore it is written also in the Law, "Thou shalt not revile thy
gods, nor speak evil against the ruler of thy people." Let no one suppose
then that the Lord was speaking about idols of stone, but He calls 'gods'
those who are placed over you. Moses also said again in the Book of
Numbers, when the people had murmured against him and against Aaron,
Ex. xvi. 8 "It is not against us that ye murmur, but against the Lord God."
Luke x. 16 Also our Saviour said, "He that wrongeth you wrongeth Me, and Him that
sent Me." For what hope is there, even a little, to him who has spoken evil
things against the Bishop? or against the Deacon? For if one have called
Matt. v. 22 a layman a fool or vile (Raca), he shall be condemned by the Synagogue, as
one of those who rise up against the Christ, because he hath called his
brother vain, him in whom the Christ dwelleth, who is not vain, but filled;
or a fool him in whom dwelleth the Holy Spirit of God, the Perfecter in
all wisdom, as if he were a fool from the Spirit that dwelleth in him! If,
therefore, any one who should say one of these things to a layman be found
f. 34 b to have fallen into all this condemnation, how much [more] if one venture
to say anything against a Bishop or against a Deacon? him by whose
means the Lord hath given you the Holy Ghost, and by whose means ye
have learnt the Word and know God, and by whose means ye are known
of God, and by whose means ye are sealed; and by whose means ye are
become the sons of light; and by whose means the Lord in baptism, by
the laying on of the Bishop's hand, gave witness about each of you, and
Psalm ii. 7 caused His holy voice to be heard and said, "Thou art My son, this day
have I begotten thee." Therefore, O my son, love thy Bishops, those
by whose hands thou art become a son of God, and [1] knowest the right
Ap. Con. II. xxxiii. hand [1], and cherish him who after God is thy father and thy mother;
Ex. xxi. 17 Matt. xv. 4 for every one who mocketh his father or his mother, let him die the death.
But honour ye the Bishops who are able to loose you from sins, those who
have begotten you anew by means of water, those who have filled you
with the Holy Ghost, those who have nourished you with the Word as
with milk, those who have established you with the doctrine of life, those

[1] S. and the right hand thy mother.

who have confirmed you by admonition, and made you partakers in the
holy Eucharist of God, and made you sharers and heirs of God's promise.
Reverence these [men], and honour them (the Bishops) with all honour,
for they have received authority from God of life and death, not that
they may judge those who have sinned, and condemn them to death in
everlasting fire, excommunicating and sending away those who are condemned, may this never happen! but that they may receive and give life to
those who are converted and repent. Let these then be your Chiefs, and Ap. Con. II. xxxiv.
let them be considered by you as kings, and by deeds give honour to
them as kings, for it is required of you that ye provide for them and
for those that are with them.

For thus it is written in the first book of the Kingdoms, that Samuel f. 35 a
the prophet said unto the people by means of words of the Lord, to those
that asked from him a king, and he said unto them, "This is the law 1 Sam. viii. 11
of the king who shall reign over you; he will take your sons, and appoint
them over his chariots, and make them runners before him; and will make 12
to himself captains over thousands, and captains over hundreds; they
shall reap his harvest, and gather his vintage, and shall keep in order the
instruments of his chariots. Your daughters he shall take to be weavers, 13
and servants of his house. Your fields, and your vineyards, and your 14
olive-yards, the best, he will take and give to his servants, and to eunuchs.
Your maidservants and menservants, and your oxen and your asses he 16
shall take and tithe for the service of his work. He will take tithe of your 17
sheep; and ye also shall be his servants." According to this likeness also
the Bishop rules. For if even a king who reigned over all that multitude
of people, took from that people, as it is written in Hosea, that "the people Hos. i. 10
of the children of Israel are many as the sand that is on the shore of the
sea, which cannot be measured nor numbered," and according to the number
of that people were also the services that were required from it, thus now
also the Bishop taketh to himself from the people, those whom he considereth and knoweth to be worthy of him and of his office, and maketh them
elders and counsellers, members of his session, deacons and subdeacons, all
as he requireth according to the service of a house. What more can we
say? for the king who wears the crown, reigns only over the body, and binds
and looses only in this world, but the Bishop reigns over both soul and
body, that he may loosen on the earth, and bind in heaven, by heavenly f. 35 b
power. For it is a great heavenly power, that of the Almighty, which is
given to him. Nevertheless, love ye your Bishop as a father, reverence him
as a king, and honour him as God. Present to him your fruits, and the

work of your hands, that your firstfruits may be blessed. Give to him
your tithes, and your vows, and your oblations; from them he will require
to be nourished, and to provide also for those who are in want, to every one
as it is proper for him. Thus thy offering shall be acceptable to the Lord
thy God, for a sweet savour in the height of heaven, before the Lord thy
God, and He will bless thee, and multiply to thee the good things of His
Prov. xi. 26 promise. For it is written in Wisdom, that "every simple soul shall be
blessed," and that "blessings shall be on the head of him who giveth."
Because of this be constant in work, and labour, and bring a gift; for the
Lord hath lightened your burden, and loosened from you the chains of
fetters, and lifted from you the heavy yoke; and made Deuteronomy
pass away from you, according to the greatness of God's mercy, as it is
Is. xlix. 9 written in Isaiah, "Say to those who are in chains, Go out," and again,
Is. xlii. 7 "to bring out the prisoners from the prisons." And in David He said,
Ps. lxix. 33 that "He despiseth not His prisoners." And again in the Gospel He
Matt. xi. 28 said, "Come unto me, all ye that are weary and carry heavy burdens, and
29 I will give you rest. Take My yoke upon you, and learn of Me, for I am
30 meek and humble of heart, and ye shall find rest unto your souls; for My
f. 36 a yoke is easy, and My burden is light." If, therefore, the Lord, in the gift
Ap. Con. II. xxxv. of His goodness, hath loosed you and given you rest, and brought your
souls to enlargement, that ye be not again bound by sacrifices and by
sin-offerings, by purifications, by vows, and by gifts, by oblations, by
burnt-offerings[1], by shewbread, and by observations of purifications, again,
by tithes, and by firstfruits, and by heave offerings, and by gifts, all
these things were of necessity appointed for them to give; ye then are
not bound by these things, for it is required of you that ye know the
Matt. v. 20 word of the Lord which said, that "unless your righteousness exceed
the righteousness of the scribes and Pharisees, ye shall not enter into
the kingdom of Heaven." Thus, therefore, your righteousness is more
excellent than the tithes, and firstfruits, and heave offerings of these
Mark x. 21 people, when ye act as it is written, "Sell all that ye have, and give to
sic the poor." Therefore do thus, and keep the commandment by means of
the Bishop and the priest, and thy mediator who is with the Lord God,
for He has commanded thee to give. Take care that thou provide for
these things, and do not exact an account from the Bishop; do not
watch him as to how he provides and fulfils his stewardship, or when
he gives, or to whom or how, whether well or ill, or if he gives as is
fitting, for it is the Lord God who is the exactor, who has committed

[1] S. + by [Sabbath] rests (idleness).

this stewardship to his hands, and counted him worthy of the priesthood
of all this office. In order, therefore, that thou observe not nor require an
account from the Bishop, nor speak evil things against him, resisting God,
nor offend the Lord, let there be put before thine eyes what was said to
thee in Jeremiah, "Shall the clay say to the potter, Thou workest not, and **Is. xlv. 9**
thou hast no hands;" as he that saith to his father and his mother, "Hast **10** f. 36 b
thou brought me forth?" but labour with a single mind and work in the house
of God. Be it always written and established in thy heart, and remember **Ap. Con. II. xxxvi.**
the saving voice of the renewal of the Law, as the Lord hath said,
"Thou shalt love the Lord thy God with all thy heart, and with all thy soul, **Deut. vi. 5**
and with all thy strength." Your strength then is the property of the world.
Do not love the Lord with the lips only, like that people to whom reproving He saith, "This people honoureth Me with its lips, but its heart is far **Is. xxix. 13**
from Me." But love thou the Lord and honour Him with all thy strength; **Mark vii. 6**
and bring thy gifts at all times, and keep not away from the Church.
When thou receivest the Eucharist of the sacrifice, give whatever cometh
to thy hand, as thou partakest, to the strangers; for this is collected by the
Bishop for the reception of all strangers. Therefore according as thou
art able, put down, and keep thyself, because the Lord hath said in the
Law, "Thou shalt not appear before Me empty." Therefore do good works, **Ex. xxiii. 15**
lay up for thyself a (S. + everlasting) treasure above in Heaven where **Matt. vi. 20** *sic*
moth doth not destroy, nor thieves steal. When thou doest thus, do not
judge the Bishop, nor the layman, because to you laymen it is said, "Judge **Matt. vii. 1**
not, that ye be not judged." For if thou judgest thy brother, and accusest
him, thou considerest thy brother guilty, that is to say, thou accusest **Rom. ii. 1**
thyself; thou art then judged with the guilty; for the Bishop has the
power to judge, as it is said to them, "Be accurate discerners." It is, f. 37 a
therefore, required of the Bishop as a tester of silver that he should divide **Ap. Con. II. xxxvii.**
the evil from the good; those that are completely evil he should reject and **2 Tim. ii. 15**
throw out; but those who are hard and defective for any reason, like those
who are not defective, he should leave them in the crucible. The layman
then is not allowed to judge his neighbour, nor even to impose upon
himself a burden which is not his; for the weight of this burden belongs
not to the layman, but to the Bishop. Therefore thou, being a layman,
do not lay snares for thyself, but leave judgment in the hands of those
who will have to answer for it to the Lord. But as for thee, strive to
make peace with all men, and love thy limbs the children of thy people,
because the Lord hath said, "Love thy neighbour as thyself." **Matt. xix. 19**

CHAPTER X.

Admonition about false brethren, and investigation about those that are accusers, or witnesses against any one, and the decree of punishment against those who are convicted of sin; and the consolation and reception into the Church, if they shew repentance; and injunction to the Bishops that they give the hand and bind up those who have sinned if they repent; that they should not judge with partiality, and be convicted before God; and that they should convict him who accuses falsely, in punishing as was fit him who was accused.

If then there be false brethren, [who] on account of envy or the jealousy of enemies[1], and of Satan, who works by them, bring a false accusation against one of the brethren, or even a true one, those shall know that every one who investigates about these things, in order
f. 37 b to accuse or blaspheme about any one, he is the son of anger, and where anger is, God is not; for anger is of Satan, who by means of these false brethren never allows peace to be in the Church. Therefore when ye know them, those that are so far wanting in sense, first of all believe them not, and secondly, Bishops and Deacons, beware of them, how ye say ought of the things that ye have heard from them to any of the brethren. Consider about him against whom they bring an accusation, investigate wisely, compare his actions, and if he be found to merit reproof, according to the doctrine of our Lord which He hath spoken
Matt. xviii. 15 16 in the Gospel, reprove him between thee and him; if he repent, and be converted, save him. And if he will not be convinced, reprove him before two or three, and fulfil that which was said, that at the mouth of two or three witnesses every word shall be established; for therefore, brethren, it is required for witness, that it stand upon the mouth of two or three witnesses, because the Father, and the Son, and the Holy Ghost testify about the works of men; for where there is admonition of doctrine, there is also discipline and conversion of those who have wandered. Therefore at the mouth of two or three witnesses every word shall be
Ap. Con. II. xxxviii. Matt. xviii. 17 established. And if he obey not, reprove him before all the Church; if he do not hear even the Church, let him be counted unto thee as a heathen and as a publican. Because the Lord hath said unto you, O Bishops, that henceforth ye receive not that man into the Church [2]as Christians[2] and be not partakers with him; for not even the heathen or the wicked

[1] S. the Enemy.

[2] S. as a Christian

publicans dost thou receive into the Church, nor make thyself partaker
with them, unless they first repent, promising so that they may believe, f. 38 a
and never henceforth again do evil deeds; for therefore our Lord and
Saviour gave room for repentance to those who have sinned; for even Ap. Con. II. xxxix.
I Matthew, who am one of the twelve Apostles, who speak to you by
this Didascalia, I was a publican of old, and because I believed, grace
came upon me, and I repented from my former works, and I was thought
worthy to become an Apostle and a preacher of the Word of God. Again
also John [1]the Baptist[1], that he might seek, preached in the Gospel to
publicans, not to cut off their hope, but taught them how they should act
in future. When they asked him for a reply he said to them, "Do not Luke iii. 13
exact more than what is commanded and appointed for you." And also
Zacchæus in repentance the Lord received, making a request of him. We
do not refuse salvation even to the heathen if they repent and renounce
and remove from themselves their error. Therefore let him be accounted
to you as a heathen and as a publican, he who is convicted of evil works
and of falsehood; and afterwards if he promise to repent as the heathen,
when they wish and promise to repent and say, "We believe," we receive
them into the congregation that they may hear the Word, but we do
not communicate with them until they receive the seal and are confirmed.
Thus also we do not communicate with these until they shew the fruits
of repentance; for they can certainly come in, if they wish to hear the
Word, that they may not perish utterly, but in prayer they take no part,
but go outside; because that even they, when they see that they do f. 38 b
not take part in the Church, restrain themselves, and repent of their
former deeds, and become eager to be received into the Church in prayer.
They also who see them and hear that they have gone out like publicans
may fear, and take heed to themselves that they sin not, lest it happen
thus to them also, and they go out of the Church, being reproved for
sin or for falsehood. Do not utterly prevent them then from entering Ap. Con. II. xl.
the Church, and hearing the discourse of the Bishop; for even our Lord
and Saviour did not completely reject and cast out the publicans and
sinners, but even ate with them. Because of this also the Pharisees
murmured against Him, saying, "He eateth and drinketh with publicans Mark ii. 16
and sinners." Then our Saviour answered and said against their
thoughts and murmurings, "They that are whole have no need of a 17
physician, but they that are sick." Therefore have intercourse with those
who have been reproved for their sins, and are in a bad state, and

[1] S. the prophet

attach them to you, and take care of their [interests], and talk ye with them and console them, keep hold of them, and cause them to be
Ap. Con. II. xli. converted; and afterwards when every one of them has repented, and has shewn the fruits of repentance, thereafter receive him in prayer as [ye do] to the heathen. As therefore thou baptizest a heathen, and thereafter receivest him, so on that man also lay the hand, every one praying for him; thereafter bring him in and let him partake with the Church. Let that laying on of the hand be to him instead of baptism; for if by the laying on of the hand and by baptism they receive the communication
f. 39 a of the Holy Ghost...therefore as a sympathetic physician sharing in suffering, heal all those who have sinned, and distribute with all wisdom, offer healing for the help of their lives; and be not ready to cut off the members of the Church, but make use of the Word of remedies, also of admonitions of preparation[1] and of the plasters of supplication; for if an ulcer goes deep, and diminishes his flesh, by means of curative medicines nourish it, and reduce it. If there be in it foulness, by a sharp medicine, that is to say by the word of reproof, purify it; and if more flesh should spring up, by a harsh medicine, that is to say, by the communication of judgment shave it off and reduce it. If there be in it gangrene, burn it with a cautery, that is to say, with the incision of a long fast, cut off the putridness of the ulcer. If the ulcer grow and get the better of the cauteries, decide about that which is corrupt, then after much consultation with other physicians cut off that member which is corrupt that it destroy not all the body. Be not ready to amputate speedily, and do not rush in a hurry and run to the saw of many teeth, but first use scalpels, and cut the ulcer, that the cause of the evil which is hidden inside it may be seen openly and be known, that the whole body may be kept from being affected. But if thou see a person who does not wish to repent, but has completely cut off hope of himself, then with grief and sorrow cut him off and cast him out of the Church.
f. 39 b Ap. Con. II. xliii. For if thou findest that that accusation of calumny is false, and ye pastors with the Deacons have received the falsehood as truth, because of the accepting of persons, or because of offerings which ye have received; and ye change judgments, because ye wish to do the will of the Evil one, and him who is accused, being guiltless of this accusation, ye put out and cast him from the Church, ye will give an account in the day of
Deut. i. 17 the Lord; for it is written, "Thou shalt not respect persons in judgment,"
Ex. xxiii. 8 and again the Scripture hath said, that a "bribe blindeth the eyes of seers,

[1] S. emollients

and perverteth righteous words." And again it hath said, "Deliver the Is. i. 17
oppressed, judge the orphans, justify the widows"; and judge righteous judgment in the gates. Take heed then that ye be not respecters of persons and be condemned by the word of the Lord, who hath spoken thus,
"Woe unto those that make bitter sweet, and sweet bitter; and call light Is. v. 20 *sic*
darkness, and darkness what is bright, and justify the wicked for his 23
reward, and pass over the righteousness of the righteous." But be watchful, that ye condemn not any one iniquitously, and help the wicked, because that in condemning others ye are condemning yourselves; as
the Lord hath said, that "with what judgment ye judge ye shall be judged, Luke vi. 37
and as ye condemn, ye shall be condemned." Therefore remember *sic*
and apply to yourselves this word, "Forgive, and it shall be forgiven you; condemn not, and ye shall not be condemned." If then, your judgment, O Bishops, be without respect of persons, look at him who is the accuser of his brother, if he be a false brother, if for the sake of envy or jealousy or calumny he have brought disturbance on the Church of God, and he should kill him who is calumniated by him, being put out f. 40 a of the Church and delivered to the destruction of fire; thou therefore judge him severely, because he has brought an evil thing against his brother, as it were from his own imagination; if he had not found that it goes before to [1]his hearing[1]; he would have killed his brother in the fire; for it
is written, that "every one who sheddeth man's blood, his blood shall be shed Gen. ix. 6
for the blood which he hath shed." When that one then is found out to be *sic* Ap. Con.
thus, put him out of the Church with a great reprimand as a murderer; II. xliii.
and after a time, if he promise to repent, admonish him, and lay a hard discipline upon him; and thereafter put on [your] hand and receive him into the Church; and take heed and observe him that is such, lest again it happen against some one else. And if ye see him after he has entered the Church, that again he quarrels and wishes to accuse others also, and chatters and fabricates, and casts blame upon many falsely: put him out, that he may never again disturb and trouble the Church; for he that is such, even if he be within, because he is not suitable to the Church, is of no advantage to her. For we see that there are men who are born with superfluous things in their bodies, let us say fingers or any other superfluous flesh; those people then that have such things according to the flesh, it is a disgrace and a shame to them, both to the flesh and to the man, because he has too much of them. When they are taken away by a practitioner, that man receives beauty

[1] S. the hearing of the judge

and loveliness of flesh, and nothing is wanting to it, on account of that superfluity that has been taken away from him, but he is even the more
f. 40 b seen in his beauty for it. In like manner therefore, ye also, O pastors, conduct yourselves; because the Church is a body, the members being we who believe in God, and are in love in the fear of the Lord according to the commandment of the tradition which we have received. Therefore he that devises evil things against the Church, and troubles its members, and loves the blames and accusations of enemies[1], that is to say, turmoils and contentions and calumnies and murmurings and quarrels and questions and incrimination and afflictions and accusations; he that loves these things and makes them, and moreover the Enemy is working in him, and he remains in the Church, is a stranger to the Church, and of the household of the Enemy, for it is him whom he serves, who works in him, and he offends and afflicts the Church; that one then if he remains within, is a disgrace to the Church because of his blasphemies (S. + and his great agitation, and there is danger lest he destroy the Church of God). To that one
Prov. xxii. 10 therefore do as it is written in Wisdom, "Cast out the evil man from the congregation, and his contention shall go out with him"; on account of litigation and reproach, that he sit not in the congregation and disgrace them all. For that one, when he goes out for the second time from the Church, is justly cut off, and the Church is the more beautified, for there is peace in it (S. + for it was wanting to her, because from that hour the Church will be free from blasphemy and trouble).... But if your mind be not pure, either on account of respect of persons, or on account of gifts of filthy lucre which ye have received, and ye put out of the Church those who walk correctly, and ye increase many evil, quarrelsome persons, and profligate rulers amongst you, ye bring blasphemy against the assembly of the Church, and ye bring danger of death upon yourselves, that ye be deprived of eternal life, because ye have pleased man, and turned from the truth of God, for the sake of respecting persons, and for the sake
f. 41 a of accepting vain gifts; and ye have scattered the Catholic Church, daughter and beloved of the Lord God.

CHAPTER XI.

Again, exhortation to Bishops and Deacons, that they govern justly, and that they be with one another in concord and love; that they do not receive testimony from the heathen against a believer, and that a Christian be not vexed and contend with his neighbour. If it happen that they have a lawsuit, let them not say their say before the heathen, but before the Church, and let

[1] S. the Enemy.

them be pacified, even if one of them lose something according to the flesh; and let him that is hard and obstinate about peace be kept from the Church until he repent; when the two persons approach, let those judge who judge without respect of persons, with much caution, on Monday, investigating the conduct of him who brings the accusation, and his conscience, and the reason of his lawsuit and contention. And him that is accused in like manner. Let them punish justly him that is found guilty.

Again, about those who are angry, that it is right they should forgive each other's faults, if it be that we seek forgiveness from God.

Strive therefore, O Bishops, with the Deacons, that ye be righteous before the Lord, because the Lord hath said, "If ye be righteous with Me, I also will be righteous with you; and if ye walk with Me frowardly, I also will walk frowardly, saith the Lord of Hosts." Be ye therefore righteous, that ye may be worthy to receïve praise from the Lord[1]. Let therefore both the Bishops and the Deacons be of one mind, and let them feed the people carefully in one opinion. For it is required of you twain that ye be one flesh, father and son, for ye are in the likeness of the Divinity. Let the Deacon make known everything to the Bishop, as the Christ doth to His Father; let the Deacon settle some of them himself that he can; the rest of the other things the Bishop must judge; but nevertheless let the Deacon be the ear of the Bishop, and his mouth and his heart, and even his soul; for when ye twain are of one mind and in one consent there is peace in the Church. This praise then becomes the Christian, that he have not an evil word with any one. But if some temptation should happen to some one from the operation of the Enemy, and he have a lawsuit, let him strive to be delivered from it, even if he lose somewhat by it. Only let him not go to the judgment of the heathen, and do not ye receive the testimony of the heathen about any of our people, for by means of the heathen the Enemy plots against the servants of God. Because the heathen are destined to stand on the left, he calls them the left, for our Lord hath said to us thus, "Let not thy left hand know what thy right hand doeth." Let not then the heathen know anything about your lawsuits, and receive not testimony against yourselves from them. Be not judged before them, as also it is said in the Gospels, "Give to Caesar that which is Caesar's, and to God that which is God's." Be therefore willing to lose, and more zealous to make peace though losing somewhat in worldly matters for the sake of peace; before God it will be thy gain, because thou fearest

2 Sam. xxii. 27 *sic* Ps. xviii. 26 *sic*

Ap. Con. II. xliv.

f. 41 b

Ap. Con. II. xlv.

Ap. Con. II. xlvi.

Matt. vi. 3

Luke xx. 25

[1] S. + and not the blame which is its opposite

God, and doest according to the commandment. But if there be brethren who have an unavoidable quarrel with one another, which God forbid! it is required of you [1]that ye immediately make peace[1], that ye rulers may know that those who venture to act thus perform no act of brotherhood in the Lord. If then one of them be of the children of God, humble and much oppressed, that one is a son of light; but he who is hard and bold and injurious and a blasphemer, he is a hypocrite (S. + and the Enemy is working through him). Reprove him therefore, and
f. 42 a reprimand him, disgrace him and put him out of the Church as a rebel, and afterwards receive him that he may not perish utterly. When ye punish and rebuke those that are such, ye will not have many lawsuits. For if they do not know the word which was spoken by our Lord in
Matt. xviii. 21 the Gospel, about how many times, if my brother offend me, shall I forgive him? and they are angry with one another (S. + and become enemies), teach them, and make peace between them, as it is said,
Matt. v. 9 "Blessed are the peacemakers." Know that it is required of the Bishop with the Elders that he judge cautiously, as our Saviour said, when they[2]
Matt. xviii. 21 asked Him about how often, if my brother offend me, shall I forgive
22 him? until seven times? But our Lord said, Not until seven times, but until seventy times seven seven. For thus the Lord desireth, that those who are His own in truth, should never have aught against any, and
Ap. Con. II. xlvii. should not be angry with any one[3]. But if there happen anything, by the operation of the Enemy, let them be judged before you; let it be on Monday, lest it happen that some one rise up against the word of your judgments; that there be opportunity for you until the Sabbath, that ye may arrange the matter, and make peace, and pacify them on the Sunday. Let the Bishops then be constant in all judgments with the Elders and Deacons, and judge ye without respect of persons; the two individuals therefore coming and standing together in judgment, as the
Col. iii. 13 Scripture hath said, "Those who have any controversy or litigation with one another," and when ye have heard them righteously, give an answer of judgment. Strive to keep them in love, before the judgment come out against them, (S. + lest against one of them being a brother there come among you a condemnation of earthly judgment, but judge thus, even as ye shall certainly be judged), so that in the judgment ye may have the Christ as Associate, Counsellor, Assessor and Overseer of the Court.
f. 42 b If there are people against whom an accusation is brought that they

[1] S. om. [2] S. we

[3] S. + and should still less have lawsuits with any one

do not walk well in the way of the Lord, having heard the two individuals,
investigate carefully, like people who decree judgment concerning eternal
life, or for a harsh and bitter death; and if some one be reproved and
go out of the Church, he is cast out from life and from everlasting
glory...he is rejected by men, and found guilty before God. (S. + There- Ap. Con.
fore judge according to the gravity of that conviction with much II. xlviii.
clemency), and incline a little, that ye may save, without respect of
persons, (S. + rather than cause to perish, when ye have condemned
those who are judged). But if there be a man who is innocent, and is
condemned by judges from respect of persons, it will not hurt him
before God (S. + the judgment of unjust judges) but will rather advantage
him the more on account of the short time that he hath been unjustly
judged by men. (S. Afterwards in the day of judgment, because he
was unjustly condemned, he will be the judge of the unjust judges,
for ye have been mediators of unjust judgments.) Therefore thus shall ye
receive retribution from God, and ye shall be cast out of the Catholic
Church of God, and that shall be accomplished against you that by
the judgment that ye have judged ye shall be judged. Therefore when Ap. Con.
ye sit to judge, let the two individuals come and stand together; we do II. xlix.
not call them brethren until there be peace betwixt them; and investigate
carefully with diligence between them about those things concerning
which they have a lawsuit and contention with one another. Learn first
about him who accuses if there be any accusation against him, or if he
have brought actions also against others, and again [if] the accusation
proceed from some former enmity, or from contention or envy, and
what his conduct is, and if he be humble and without anger; if he
love widows, and the poor, and strangers, and doth not love filthy lucre;
if he be quiet and philanthropic, a lover of all men; if he be merciful,
and stretch out his hand to give; not a glutton and not greedy; not
avaricious and not a drunkard; for a perverse heart that deviseth evil Prov. vi.
things disturbeth cities (S. + at all times), even if he have not done the 14 f. 43 a
evil things that are in the world (S. + adultery, and fornication, and other
such things). If then he who accuses be free from all these things,

(S. + from of old it is known and manifest that he is a believer and his accusation Ap. Con.
truthful; but if it be known that he is perverse and quarrelsome, and that his II. l.
deeds are unrighteous, it is evident that he hath brought false witness against your
brother. When, therefore, it is found and known that he is unjust; reprove
him and put him out for a time; until he repent and be converted and weep;
lest again he blaspheme against any other person among the brethren who conducts
himself well; or lest another who is like him, sitting in your assembly and seeing

that he is not reproved, venture also and do likewise to one of the brethren, and perish from before God; but if he who has sinned be reproved and punished, and go out for a time, he also who is ready to be like him and to act like him, when he sees him put out, may also fear, lest it happen to him in like manner; and he will submit, and live before God, and not be ashamed at all before man. Also in regard to him who is accused, take counsel likewise, and consider amongst yourselves, and observe his habits and deeds in the world, whether ye have heard many accusations against him, or whether many wicked things are done by him; if it be found that many evil deeds are wrought by him, it appears as if also this accusation that they bring against him were true. It may also happen, that some sin has formerly been committed by him, but that he is innocent from the present accusation. Therefore investigate carefully about these things; that with great caution and with truth you pronounce sentence of judgment. Against him that is found guilty judge righteously, and pronounce judgment against him; but he amongst them who doth not stand by your judgment, let him be reproved, and let him go out of the assembly, until he repent, and implore the Bishop or the Church, and confess that he has sinned and that he repents; and thus there will be a help to many, lest even, when another person sees him sitting in the Church neither rebuked nor punished, he also venture to do like him, thinking that he will live before men, but before
Ap. Con. II. li. God he will perish. But if ye hear one person alone, the other not standing,
nor defending himself on account of the action which they bring against him, but ye pronounce judgment hastily without consultation or investigation, and condemn according to false words which ye believe, he not having stood nor made any defence on his own behalf and ye have condemned him, ye have become partakers before God with him that hath brought the false witness, and ye shall be punished with him before God; for the Lord hath said in the
Prov. xxvi. 17 Proverbs, that "he who stirs up strife that is not his is like him that taketh hold of
John vii. 24 the tail of a dog." In another place He hath said, "Judge righteous judgment"; and
Is. i. 17 again He hath said, "Judge the orphans, and justify the widows," and again He
Is. lviii. 6 saith, "Let the oppressed go free, and loose every unjust bond." But if it be
that ye resemble those Elders that were in Babylon, who brought false witness against Susan, and condemned her unjustly to death, ye also will be partakers in their judgment and condemnation. For the Lord saved Susan by means of Daniel from the hand of the unjust; (S. f. 40 b) but these Elders who were guilty of her blood He condemned to the fire. Then let those who are of the sanctuary be far removed from the things of the world. Nevertheless
Ap. Con. II. lii. we say that ye [must] see, brethren, when murderers are brought before
the Authority, that the judges question carefully those that have brought them, and learn from them what they have done, and then again they say to that doer of evil things, if these things are so, and he confess and say yea, they send him not at once to die, but again they interrogate him for many days, and draw the curtains, and consider and consult much together, and then at last pass sentence of death upon him, and lift up their hands to Heaven, and call to witness that we are clear from men's blood; for they do these things being yet heathen, and knowing not God nor that they shall receive retribution from God on account of those whom they

judge and condemn unjustly. But ye, knowing who our God is, and what are His judgments, do ye dare to pronounce sentence on one who is not guilty? We therefore counsel you to investigate carefully with much caution, because that the sentence of judgment which ye pronounce goeth up to God at once; and if ye have judged justly, ye will receive the reward of justice from God, both now and in that [world] which is to come; and if ye have judged unjustly, thus also shall ye receive retribution from God. Strive therefore, brethren, that ye be found worthy to receive praise from God, and not blame, because praise from God is everlasting life to men, but blame from God is everlasting death to men.) **Ap. Con. II. liii.**

Be careful therefore, O Bishops, that ye be not hasty in sitting down in judgment hurriedly, lest ye oppress and condemn any one; but before they come and stand in judgment, bring them together, and make peace between them; and admonish them that have the lawsuit and strife with one another; and teach them first that no one ought to be angry; for
the Lord hath said, that "every one who is angry with his brother [1]without **Matt. v.**
cause[1] is condemned in the judgment"; and again, that if it happen that there is anger by the work of the Enemy, it is required of you immediately in that day that ye be reconciled and pacified, and that ye be at peace
with one another; for it is written, "Let not the sun go down upon **Eph. iv. 26**
wrath against thy brother." David also said, "Be ye angry, and sin not." *sic* **Ps. xxxvii. 8**
This is, that ye be quickly reconciled, lest anger remaining, there be a
grudge with it, and it should bear sin, for it is said in the Proverbs, "The **Prov. xix. 16**
soul that keepeth a grudge shall die." Again, also our Saviour said, "If thou **Matt. v. 23**
bring thy gift to the altar, and there rememberest that thy brother keepeth
anger against thee; leave thy gift before the altar, and go, first be **24**
reconciled to thy brother, and then come, offer thy gift." But the gift of God is our prayer and our Eucharist. If it be then that thou hast some grudge against thy brother, or he against thee, thy prayer is not heard, nor thy Eucharist accepted, but thou art found void of prayer and
of the Eucharist, because of the anger that thou keepest. Prayer ought f. 43 b
to be made diligently at every season. But those who are in anger and malice with their brethren, God heareth them not. If then thou prayest three times an hour, thou hast no advantage, for thou art not heard because of the enmity towards thy brother. Therefore if thou carest, and strivest to be a Christian, acquiesce in the word of the Lord which He spake.
"Loose all the bonds of wickedness, cut the bonds of the yoke of avarice"; **Is. lviii. 6**
for our Saviour hath given thee this authority, to forgive thy brother who hath wronged thee, until seventy times over seven, seven, that is 490 times. How many times therefore hast thou forgiven thy brother, that thou

[1] S. om.

dost not wish again to forgive him, but keepest a grudge and cherishest enmity, and desirest to go to law; thy prayer therefore is hindered, even if thou fulfil the 490 times which thou hast forgiven him, increase also for thine own sake, and in thy goodness without anger forgive thy brother. If thou doest it not for thy brother's sake, consider, and do it for thine own sake: forgive thy neighbour, that thou mayest be heard when thou prayest,
Ap. Con. II. liv. and mayest bring an acceptable offering to the Lord. Because of this therefore, O ye Bishops, that your gifts and prayers may be received, when ye stand in the church to pray, let the Deacon say with a loud voice, Is there any one who is keeping any grudge against his fellow? If there be found any people who have a lawsuit and strife with one another, persuade and make peace betwixt them; in the house as they
f. 44 a go in and say, Peace be to this house; they are also evangelists of peace who bring peace. If therefore thou preachest peace to others, it is required yet more of thee, that thou be at peace with thy brethren, as a son of light and of peace. Be to every one light and peace; and do not contend with any one, but be at rest and at peace with every one, and be a helper with God (S. + so that the number of the saved may be increased), for this is the will of the Lord God. They who love to be in enmity and quarrels, those are the enemies of God, because that the Lord
Ap. Con. II. lv. from the beginning from generation to generation, by means of prophets and righteous men, calleth to repentance and to life. And we too, the Apostles, who have been found worthy to be witnesses of His revelation in (S. + and preachers of) the knowledge of the Divine Word, we have heard from the mouth of the Lord Jesus the Christ, we know truly and say, what is His will and the will of His Father, that
Ap. Con. II. lvi. no one should perish, but that all men should believe and live; for this is
Matt. vi. 10 what He taught us, that we should say when we pray, "Thy will be done on earth as it is in Heaven," that as the Angels of Heaven and all the Powers praise God, thus also upon the earth should men praise God. It is His will therefore to save all men, and this is His delight, that there should be many who are saved. But he who is contentious, and is an enemy to his neighbour, diminishes the people of God (S. + for he sends out him whom he accuses from the Church and diminishes it) and deprives God of the soul of a man which would have been saved, or by means of his contentiousness expels and casts himself out from the Church, and thus again he sins against
Matt. xii. 30 God, for God our Saviour hath said thus, "Every one that is not with Me is
Luke xi. 23 against Me, and every one that gathereth not with Me scattereth abroad."
f. 44 b Thou art not therefore a helper with God, to gather the people, because

thou art a disturber, and a scatterer of the flock, and an adversary of God. Be not therefore constantly prone to quarrel, either by fights or by calumnies, or by enmity or by lawsuits, that thou scatter not people from the Church, because that we, by the power of the Lord God, have collected from all peoples, and from all tongues, and have brought [them] to the Church by much labour and toil, and by daily danger, that we may do the will of God, and fill the chamber with guests, that is to say, the Catholic Church, that they should be glad and rejoice and confess and praise God, Him who has called them to salvation, and ye therefore, O ye laity! be at peace with one another, and like wise doves, strive to fill the Church, and those who are without convert and reconcile and cause to enter her (the Church). This is a great reward which is promised by God, if ye save them from the fire and bring them into the Church, confirmed and believing.

CHAPTER XII.

Commands Bishops to be quiet and humble, far removed from all harshness and anger, and teaches them about the Order of the House of God, and how the places in it should be distributed for standing and for sitting, to every rank as befits it. And if there come a man from another Church, let him have honour as befits him; let him be honoured with the place that suits him, and let not the Christ, who loveth strangers, be despised in him.

Ye then, O Bishops, be not harsh nor tyrannical nor irascible; and **Ap. Con. II. lvii.** be not wroth with the people of God whom He has given into your hands; do not destroy the House of God nor scatter His people; but convert f. 45 a all men, that ye may be helpers with God. Assemble the believers with much humility and long suffering, and with patience without anger; by doctrine and entreaty, as servants of the everlasting kingdom; in your assemblies, in the holy Churches, after all good patterns form your gatherings, and arrange the places for the brethren carefully with all sobriety. Let a place be reserved for the Elders in the midst of the eastern part of the House, and let the throne of the Bishop be placed amongst them; let the Elders sit with him; but also at the other eastern side of the house let the laymen sit; for thus it is required that the Elders should sit at the eastern side of the house with the Bishops, and afterwards the laymen, and next the women: that when ye stand to pray the rulers may stand first, afterwards the laymen, and then the women also, for towards the East it is required that ye should pray, as ye know that it is written, "Give praise to God, who rideth on the heavens of heavens **Ps. lxviii 33**

towards the East." As for the Deacons, let one of them stand constantly
over the gifts of thankfulness (the Eucharist), and let another stand
outside the door and look at those who come in; and afterwards when ye
make offerings, let them serve together in the Church. And if a man
be found sitting out of his place, let the Deacon who is within reprove
him, and make him get up and sit in the place that befits him, for our
Lord compared the Church to a fold. For as we see the irrational beasts,
f. 45 b we mean oxen, sheep, and goats, lying down in herds, rising and
feeding and mating, and none of them is separate from its race; and also
the beasts of the deserts go in the mountains along with those who are like
them. Thus therefore it ought to be also in the Church, that those who
are children should sit by themselves, if there be room; if not, let them
stand upon their feet. And let those who are advanced in years sit by
themselves. But let the children stay at one side, or let their fathers
and mothers keep them beside them and let them stand on their feet.
Again, also let those who are girls sit apart, or if there be not room let
them stand on their feet behind the women. Let those who are married
and young and have children stay by themselves, but the old women and
widows sit by themselves, the Deacon seeing as every one enters that
he goes to his place, lest any one sit in a place that is not his. Let the
Deacon also notice lest any one whisper, or sleep or laugh or make signs;
for thus it is required that [people] be attentive in the Church, with watch-
fulness and good manners, and with their ears open to the word of the
Ap. Con. Lord. If there come a person from another assembly, a brother or a
II. lviii. sister, let the Deacon ask and learn if she be the wife of a man, or again
if she be a believing widow, if she be a daughter of the Church, or if it
be one of the heresies, and then let him lead her and put her in the place
that befits her. If an Elder come from another assembly, ye Elders
receive him to a share in your place, and if he be a Bishop let him sit
with the Bishop, and let him give him the honour of his place like himself;
f. 46 a and let the Bishop say to him that he preach to his people; for entreaty
and admonition of strangers is of great help, especially because it is written,
Luke iv. 24 that "no prophet is acceptable in his country." When ye are offering
the Eucharist, let him speak. If he be wise, and give thee honour and do
not wish to officiate, yet over the cup let him speak. If while ye are sitting,
there come another person, either man or woman who has honour in
the world, either from the place or from another assembly, thou then,
O Bishop, who speakest the word of the Lord, or hearest, or readest,
do not shew respect to persons and leave off the service of thy word

to appoint them a place, but remain thou quietly as thou art; do not interrupt thy word, but let the brethren receive them. If there be no room, let that one of the brethren who is full of love, and loves his brethren and would do honour, rise and give them place. Let him stand on his feet. If while the boys or the girls are sitting, he or she that is eldest rise and give up his [or her] place, look thou, O Deacon, at those who are sitting, for him who is younger than his comrades or her who is younger; make them rise, and seat the one who rose and gave up his place. Lead the one whom thou hast made to rise and put him behind his comrades, that others also may be educated and learn to give place to those who are more honourable than they. If a poor man or a poor woman come, either belonging to thine own assembly, or from another assembly, and especially if they are advanced in years, and there be no room for such, appoint a place for them with all thy heart, O Bishop, even if thou hast to sit on the floor, and be not thou like a respecter of persons, but let thy f. 46 b
service be acceptable to God.

CHAPTER XIII.

That no Christian should neglect the assembly of the Church at the time of prayer, or of the Eucharist; not for the sake of the work of the hands, or any other work of the world; he should not go to a theatrical spectacle, to hear heathen words, dissuading his soul away from the hearing of the words of the Scriptures of life; nor to the foreign assemblies of heretics. Let those who are children in the Church hear and serve in it without laziness. Let no Christian love idleness from the work of handicraft, which is alien to the Church.

When thou teachest, command and remind the people, that they **Ap. Con. II. lix.**
be constant in the assembly of the Church; so that ye be not hindered, but that they be constantly assembled, that no one diminish the Church by not assembling, and make smaller by a member the body of Christ. For it is not about others alone that a man should think, but also about himself, hearing what our Lord hath said, that "he who gathereth not with Me scattereth **Matt. xii. 30**
abroad." As, therefore, ye are members of the Christ, scatter not yourselves from the Church by not assembling yourselves, for ye have a head, that is the Christ, as He counsels and promises, that ye are partakers with us. Therefore do not despise yourselves, and do not deprive our Saviour of His members; do not mangle and scatter His body, do not have more respect to the affairs of the world than to the word of God, but leave everything on the Lord's day and run eagerly towards your Church, for this is your glory.

If not, what excuse will ye have before God, for those who have not
f. 47 a assembled on the Lord's day, to hear the Word of Life, and to be nourished
Ap. Con. II. lx. with the divine food which endureth for ever? For ye strive to get the
things that are for a time, for a day or an hour, but ye neglect those that
are eternal; ye go on providing for bathing, for eating, for drinking, for the
belly, and for other things to be nourished; but for eternal things ye do not
care; ye despise your souls and do not hasten to the Church, that ye may
hear and receive the Word of God. In comparison with those who err, what
apology have ye? for, because the heathen, when they rise from their sleep
every day, go in the morning to worship and serve their idols, before all their
works and labours they go first and worship their idols, and also they do not
neglect their feasts and pilgrimages, but assemble constantly, not only the
natives, but also those who come from afar. They also assemble for the
spectacle of their own theatre, and all of them come. Thus also those who
vainly are called Jews, are idle one day for six, and assemble in their
synagogue. They do not neglect their holidays, they who have deprived
themselves of the strength of the Word, because they believe not, nor even
of the name by which they have called themselves, *i.e.* Jews. Jew is
interpreted as confession, but they are not confessors, for they do not confess
to the murder of the Christ, which they have committed in transgressing the
Law, that they may repent and live. If, therefore, those who are not saved
strive always for the things in which there is no profit nor help to them,
f. 47 b what excuse has he before the Lord God? he who restrains himself from
the assembly of the Church, and does not even imitate the Gentiles; and
because he does not assemble, neglects himself and goes afar, and does
Jer. xvi. 11 iniquities; those to whom the Lord spake by means of Jeremiah, "My
laws ye have not kept;" but ye have not even walked according to the
laws of the Gentiles, and ye have almost excelled them in wickedness.
Jer. ii. 11 "Have the nations changed their gods, which yet are no gods? but My
people hath changed its glory for that which doth not profit." How then
can he who is neglectful make excuse, he who is not zealous in the
Ap. Con. II. lxi. assembling of the Church of God? If a man gets an excuse on account of
secular work and is prevented, let him know that the handicrafts of believers
are called works of superfluity; for the sure work is the fear of God.
Do your handicrafts, therefore, as a work of superfluity for your nourishment, but let your real work be the worship of God. Strive, therefore,
never to be hindered from the assembling of the Church. But if a man
forsake the assembling of the Church of God, and go to the assembly of
the Gentiles, what shall he say, and what excuse will he make to God in

the day of judgment? who has left the Holy Church, and the words of the living God which live and give life, and can redeem and save from the fire and give life? and hath gone to the assembly of the heathen, because he desired the spectacle of the theatre? Therefore he will be considered as one of those who enter there because he desired to hear and receive the fables of their words, which are those of dead men, and of the spirit of Satan; for they are dead and cause death, they cause people to turn from the faith, and bring near to everlasting fire. Yet ye care for the world, and f. 48 a
occupy yourselves with domestic concerns, and ye disdain to hasten to the Catholic Church, the beloved daughter of the Lord God Most High, that ye may receive the doctrine of God which remaineth for ever and is able to give life to those who receive the Word of Life. Be, therefore, constant in assembling with the believers who are saved in your mother the Church, her who liveth and giveth life to her children. Be watchful not to assemble Ap. Con. II. lxii.
yourselves as[1] those who perish in the theatre, which is an assembly of the heathen of error and of perdition; for he who enters into the assembly of the Gentiles shall be counted as one of them, and shall receive woe; for the Lord saith by means of Isaiah the Prophet to those who are such, "Woe, woe, to [those who] come from the spectacle," and again He saith, "[2] Women who come from the spectacle, because this is a people who have Is. xxvii. 11 *sic*
no understanding." Therefore He calls the Church[3] women, those whom He has called, and brought out, and drawn from the spectacle of the theatre, and He holds and receives them, and He has taught us not to go there any more; for He saith in Jeremiah, "Learn not the way of the Jer. x. 2
nations," and again in the Gospel He hath said, "Go not in the way Matt. x. 5
of the Gentiles." Here, therefore, He teaches and warns, that we remove completely from all heresies, which are the cities of the Samaritans, and that we should not enter into strange synagogues, and[4] from their pilgrimages which are on behalf of idols. Let a believer not approach their pilgrimage, excepting to buy provision for his body and his life. Remove yourselves far from all vain spectacles of idols, and from their feasts and pilgrimages. Let then those who are children in the Church serve Ap. Con. II. lxiii.
diligently without laziness, in all things that are required, with much f. 48 b
modesty and chastity. All ye believers, therefore, at all times always when ye are not in the Church be constant at your labours; and in all the course of your life either be constant in exhortation, or labour at your work and never be idle, because the Lord hath said, "Be like the ant, O sluggard, Prov. vi. 6

[1] S. with
[2] S. + Thou wilt have mercy on
[3] S. Churches
[4] S. + let us flee also far from the theatre and

7 emulate its ways, and learn from it; for it has no office, and no one
8 to impel it, nor is it under authority. It gathers its food in the summer,
8a and collects much food in the harvest." And again He saith, "Go to the
bee, and learn how she works, that she doeth her work with wisdom, and
8b from her work she offereth food to the rich and to the poor. She is
beloved and honoured, and yet she hath little strength. She honoureth
9 wisdom and she is illustrious. Until when wilt thou sleep, O sluggard,
10 and when wilt thou arise from thy slumber? Thou wilt sleep a little and
slumber a little, and sit a little, and put thy hands upon thy breast.
11 Poverty shall come upon thee as one who runs, and want as a skilful man.
If then (S. + thou art) without laziness, thy revenues shall increase and
overflow like a fountain, and poverty be removed from thee." Work,
therefore, at all times, for idleness is a blot for which there is no cure. "If any man among you work not, neither let him eat," for the Lord even hateth sluggards, for a sluggard cannot be a believer.

2 Thess. iii. 10

CHAPTER XIV.

About Widows, and about the time of their order in the Church. Encomium on her who keeps the statute of her widowhood before God, and condemnation of her who tramples on her statute. Exhortation to the Bishop about the Widows and the Poor and the Needy.

f. 49 a

Ap. Con. III. i.

Let widows then be appointed; she who is not less than fifty years of age and over, in order that by reason of her years she may be removed from the thought of having another husband. If you appoint one who is a girl to the place of a widow, and she doth not support her widowhood because of her youth, she will take a husband, and bring disgrace upon the glory of widowhood. She will give account to God, first for having had two husbands, and next for having promised to God to be a widow; she has received as a widow and did not remain in widowhood. If there be the widow of a young man who was for a short time with her husband, and he died, [1]or for any other reason which she receives and there be no separation[1], and she remain alone by herself, being in the honour of widowhood, she will be blessed by God, because she has resembled that widow who was in Zareptah of Sidon, with whom the holy messenger, the Prophet of God, found rest, or she will be as Anna, who celebrated the coming of the Christ, and there was a testimony to her, and for her goodness she receives honour from man on the earth, and inherits glory from God in Heaven. Let not then young widows be appointed to the

Ap. Con. III. ii.

[1] S. or for any other reason there be separation

office of widows, but let them be taken care of and trained[1] lest by reason of their indigence they seek to take a husband a second time, and this act be an undisciplined one; for ye know that she who has had one husband has had him lawfully[2], and beyond this it is fornication. Therefore take by the hand those who are young, that they may remain in chastity to God. Take care of them, therefore, O Bishop, and remember also the poor; hold them by the hand, and provide for them, even if none of them be widowers or widows, and they need help on account of poverty, or of sickness, or are straitened on account of the education of their children. It is required of thee that thou care for all men, and pay attention to all men. Therefore those who bring gifts are not to give to the widows with their own hands, but are to offer to thee on their behalf, as thou art well acquainted with those who are straitened, that thou mayest distribute to them like a good steward (S. + from what is given to thee); for God knoweth him that giveth, even when he is not present; and when thou distributest tell them the name of the giver, that they may pray for him by his name. For in all the Scriptures the Lord commandeth about the poor, even that they be partakers; and He even adds in Isaiah, and saith thus, "Break thy bread to the hungry, and bring the poor man that hath no shelter into thy house; when thou seest the naked clothe him, and turn not away from thine own flesh." Therefore by every means care for the poor.

Ap. Con. III. iii.

f. 49 b

Ap. Con. III. iv.

Isaiah lviii. 7

CHAPTER XV.

How it befits Widows to conduct themselves in tranquillity and chastity, and it is not fitting that women should teach, not even those who are the Widows of the Church, nor the laity. About the dissimulation of false Widows. On the manners of chaste Widows. That it is necessary for Widows to be obedient to the Bishop and Deacons, and not to do anything without permission, and that those are guilty who act thus, or pray with those who are separated. That it is not permitted to a woman to baptize. Again, of the jealousies of false Widows amongst themselves. Reproof of those who curse by their jealousies.

It is required, therefore, of every one who is a widow that she be humble, peaceful and quiet; and also that she be not wicked nor angry, nor a great talker, nor lift up her voice when she speaks, and that she have not a long tongue, nor love quarrels; and that when she sees or hears anything that is hateful, she be as though she saw and heard it not. Let the

Ap. Con. III. v.

f. 50 a

[1] S. helped [2] S. C. + and two

widow care for nothing else, but to pray for those who give, and for the whole Church. When she is asked for an explanation by any one, let her not give an answer in haste, unless it be about righteousness alone, and about the faith of God, and let her send those who wish to be instructed to the authorities. To those who ask them, let them return an answer only. [S. + It is not fitting for a widow to teach, nor for a layman either.] But about the destruction of idols, and about there being only one God, about punishment and about rest, and about the kingdom of the name of the Christ, and about His providence, it is not incumbent on the widow nor on the layman to talk; for if they talk without the knowledge of doctrine, they bring blasphemy against the Word; for our Lord compared the word of His Gospel to a grain of mustard; for mustard, if it be not prepared with art, is bitter and sharp to those who use it. Therefore the Lord said in the

Matt. vii. 6 Gospel to widows and to all the laity, "Do not throw your pearls before swine, lest they trample them with their feet, and turn again and rend you"; for when the heathen who are instructed, hear the Word of God that it is not spoken in an orderly manner as it ought to be, for edification to eternal life, especially because it is declared to them by a woman, about how our Lord became incarnate, and about the Passion of the Christ, they

f. 50 b will mock and joke, instead of praising as is right the word of the doctrine,

Ap. Con. III. vi. and she will incur a great condemnation for the sin. Therefore it is not required nor necessary that women should be teachers, especially about the name of the Christ, and about salvation by His Passion, for women were not appointed to teach, especially not a widow, but that they should make prayer and supplication to the Lord God. For even Jesus the Christ, our Teacher, sent us the Twelve to make disciples of the people and the nations. There were with us female disciples, Mary Magdalene[1] and another Mary, and He did not send [them] to make disciples with us of the people. For if it were required that women should teach, our Teacher would have commanded them to make disciples with us. But let the widow know that she is the Altar of God, and let her constantly sit in her house; let her not wander and gad about among the houses of believers in order to receive; for the Altar of God doth not wander and gad about anywhere, but remaineth in one place. It is, therefore, not fitting that a widow should wander and gad about amongst houses; for those who are wanderers are without modesty, and do not even frequent their own houses and sit in them, because they are not widows, but blind persons, and they care for nothing else, but to be ready to receive, because they are talkative,

[1] S. + and Mary the daughter of James

and murmurers, insolent and inciters of quarrels, and they have no shame,
for those that are such are unworthy of Him who has called them, for not
even in the communion of the assembly of rest on Sunday, when they
come, are they attentive who are such, the woman or the man, they either
sleep soundly, or talk about something else; so that by their means
others also are taken captive by Satan the enemy, and he does not allow
them to be attentive to the Lord. Therefore those that are such, when they f. 51 a
enter the Church empty, go out of the Church yet more empty, because
they hear nothing that is spoken or read that they should receive it
with the ears of their hearts. Those that are such are like those about
whom Isaiah spoke, "Hear ye indeed, but understand not, and see ye Is. vi. 9
indeed, but perceive not; for the heart of this people is made fat, and 10
with their ears they hear heavily; their eyes have they closed that they
may never see with their eyes, nor hear with their ears." In this same
manner are closed the ears of the hearts of such widows, so that they sit not Ap. Con. III. vii.
beneath the shelter of their houses in order to pray and entreat the Lord,
but they hasten to run so as [to gain] some advantage, and by their talking
they accomplish the lusts of the Enemy. Such a widow then is not fitted
for the Altar of the Christ; for it is written in the Gospel, "That if two Matt. xviii. 19
agree and ask about all that they wish to be, it shall be given to you; and
if they say to a mountain, that it be removed and fall into the sea, yes, it xxi. 21
shall be thus." We see, therefore, that there are widows, by whom this
thing is considered a merchandise, and they receive with avidity, and
instead of doing good works and giving to the Bishop as for the reception
of strangers, and for the relief of the oppressed, they lend for bitter usury,
they care for nothing but Mammon, those whose gods are their purses, and
their glory is their bellies; for where their treasure is, there is also their Phil. iii. 19 Matt. vi.
heart. For she who is assiduous to gad about in order to receive does 21
not devise good things, but only worships Mammon, and serves filthy lucre; f. 51 b
and she cannot please God, nor attend to His service, by being constant
in prayer and supplication, for her soul is much held captive by diligence
in avarice. When she stands up to pray, she recollects where she should
go to receive something, or that she has forgotten again to say some word
to her friends. While she is standing in prayer her mind is not upon the
prayer, but upon the idea that has come up in her soul. The prayer of
such an one will not be heard, but is quickly cut short because of the
agitation of her mind, because she has not offered prayer to God with
her whole heart, but she goes into the thought wrought by Satan, and she
speaks with her friends about something in which there is no advantage,

because she does not know how she has believed, or of what place she is deemed worthy. But the widow who wishes to please God sits within her house, and meditates in the Lord by day and by night, without ceasing, at all times offering prayer and supplication, praying purely before the Lord, and receiving whatsoever she asketh, because all her mind is set upon this, for her soul is not greedy to receive, nor is her desire great to make great expenses, nor doth her eye wander about to see and desire anything and impede her mind. She doth not listen to wicked words to consent to them, for she goeth not out and gaddeth not without. Because of this her prayer is not impeded by anything, and her peacefulness, her quietness, with her purity, are accepted before God. Whatever she asketh of God she quickly receiveth her desire, for such a widow as she is
f. 52 a loveth not silver, nor filthy lucre, and is not greedy nor covetous, but is constant in prayer, humble, not excitable, pure and modest; who sitteth in her house and worketh with wool and flax, that she may provide something for those who are straitened, or make return to others and not receive anything from them, because she remembereth that widow to whom
Cf. Mark xii. 42 our Lord bare witness in the Gospel, her who came and threw into the
treasury two mites, which make one dinar, her whom when our Lord and
43 Teacher, the searcher of hearts, saw, He said unto us, O my disciples! this
44 poor widow hath cast in more alms than all men, because they all from their
abundance have cast in, but she hath cast in all the treasure that she had. (S. + *That it is not fitting for widows to do anything without the commandment of the Bishop.*) It is therefore required of widows to be obedient to the Bishop, to be shamefaced and modest, to reverence the Bishop as [they reverence] God; not to act according to their own will, nor to do anything except what is commanded them by the Bishop, nor talk with any one without counsel as if for conversion, nor go with any one to eat or to drink, nor should they fast with any one, nor receive aught from any one, nor put their hands upon nor pray for any one, except by the command of the Bishop; but if some one do any thing that has not been commanded let her be prevented (S. reproved) because she has conducted herself without
Ap. Con. III. viii. discipline. For whence dost thou know, O woman, from whom thou hast received, or from what service thou hast been nourished, or on account of whom thou hast fasted, or on whom thou hast put thy hand? Dost thou not know that about each of these things thou shalt give account to the
52 b Lord in the day of judgment, because thou hast been partaker of their works?

Reproof of rebellious Widows.

But thou, O widow who art without discipline, thou seest the widows thy companions, or thy brethren, in sicknesses, and thou carest not to fast and pray for thy members, to put thy hand and to visit them; but thou makest thyself as if thou wert not in health, or as if thou wert not sufficient, and with others who are in sins or who have gone out from the Church, because they give much, thou art ready to go joyfully and to visit them. Therefore ye ought to be ashamed, ye who are such, ye who wish to be wiser and more intelligent not only than men, but also more so than the Elders and the Bishops. Know then, O sisters! that in obeying all that the Pastors command you, with the Deacons, ye are obeying God, and in all that ye take part by the order of the Bishop ye are blameless before God, as also every brother of the laity, when he obeyeth the Bishop and submitteth unto him, because they will give account on behalf of all men, but if ye obey not the mind of the Bishops and the Deacons, they will be clear from your faults, and you will give account of all that you have done of your own will, or of yours, O ye widows!

It is not proper to pray with one who is censured (S. *separated*). For every one who prays or takes part with any one who has gone out of the Church, is justly reckoned with him, for these things lead to the dissolution and the destruction of souls. For if any one take part and pray with him who is censured and is put out of the Church, and doth not obey the Bishop, he obeyeth not God, and is polluted along with him. Also he f. 53a
alloweth him not to repent. For if a man doth not take part with him he repenteth, and weepeth, and prayeth, and imploreth to be received, and turneth from what he hath done and is saved.

It is not permitted to a woman to baptize.

We do not advise a woman to baptize or to be baptized by a woman, Ap. Con. III. ix.
for that is a transgression of the commandments, and there is great danger to her who baptizeth and also to him who is baptized; for if it were lawful to be baptized by a woman, our Lord and Teacher would have been baptized by Mary His mother; but He was baptized by John, as also others of the people. Therefore do not bring danger on yourselves, brothers and sisters, acting beyond the law of the Gospel.

About the jealousy of false Widows towards one another. About jealousy, Ap. Con III. xii.
or envy, or about calumny and murmurings, and about strife and vain talking, or about contention, we have spoken to you before; it is not suitable that these things should be in a Christian; nor is it fitting that one of them should even be named among the widows. But because the

Author of Evil has many devices he enters into those who are not widows,
and is glorified in them. For there are some who say of themselves that
they are widows, and do no works worthy of their name. For it is not for
the name of widowhood that they are found worthy to enter the Kingdom;
but on account of faith and works. For if she cultivate good things, she
will be honoured and praised; but if she cultivate evil things, and do
the works of the Wicked One, she shall be reproved, and cast out from
the everlasting kingdom, because she hath forsaken eternal things, and
(S. desired and) loved the things of time. For we see and hear that
there are some who are called widows and there is among them jealousy
f. 53 b of one another. For when some old woman, thy companion, has received
a garment or a gift from some one, thou, O widow, when thou seest thy
Ap. Con. III. xiii. sister comforted, thou who art a widow of God oughtest to say, Blessed
be God, who comforteth the old woman my comrade; thou wilt glorify
God, and afterwards him that gave, and thou wilt say, Let his deed be
received in truth. Remember him, Lord, for good in the day of Thy
retribution; and also my Bishop; his conduct is good before Thee, and
he dispenses alms as it is necessary. For this old woman, my comrade,
was naked, and was provided for. Increase praise to him, and give him
a crown of glory in the day of Revelation, the [day] of Thy coming.
Ap. Con. III. xiv. Again, also that widow who has received alms from the Lord shall pray for
him who served (S. did this service), hiding his name, like a wise woman,
that his righteousness[1] may be with God, and not with men. This service
Matt. vi. 3 is as it was said in the Gospel, "When thou doest alms, let not thy left
hand know what thy right hand doeth," lest when thou dost disclose and
reveal his name in praying for him who gave, his name be exposed and
come to the ears of the heathen, and the heathen, that is the men of the
left hand, should know; for it might happen also that one of the believers,
on hearing thee, should go out and talk. It is not suitable that such
things should go forth and be revealed, or be spoken of in the Church, for he
who goeth out and talketh about them obeyeth not God. But do thou
pray for him, concealing his name, and thus thou shalt fulfil that which is
written, thou and the widows that are such, who are the holy Altar of the
God, Jesus the Christ. We have now heard that there are widows who do
not conduct themselves according to the commandment, but only care for
f. 54 a this, that they may beg and wander and gad about. She again who has
received alms from the Lord, if she be without sense, revealing what has
happened (S. what is evident to her that interrogates her), reveals and

[1] =alms

makes known the name of the giver. And she, whenever she has heard it, grumbles and blames the Bishop who made the provision, or the Elder (S. Deacon) or him that gave the gift, and says, Dost thou not know that I am nearer to thee, and I am much more destitute than she? She knoweth not that this hath not happened by the will of man, but by the commandment of God. For if thou testifiest, and sayest, I am nearer to thee, and thou knowest that I am more destitute than she, thou oughtest to know him who has commanded, and be silent, and not blame him who has served; but go into thy house, and fall on thy face, and thank God on behalf of the widow thy companion, and pray also for the giver, and for the server, and seek from the Lord that the door of compassion may be opened also to thee, and the Lord will hear thy prayer quickly which is without grudge, and will send to thee more compassion than to that widow thy comrade, from whence thou hast never hoped to be served, and the proof of thy patience shall be found (S. praised). Or do ye not know that it is written
in the Gospel, "When thou doest alms, do not blow a trumpet before thee Matt. vi. 2
(S. before men), that thou mayest be seen of them, as the hypocrites do. Verily I say unto thee that they have received their reward"?

About the audacity (S. *reproof*) *of cursed Widows.*

If therefore God command that a service be performed in secret, and he who serves has performed it thus; thou therefore who hast received in secret, why dost thou proclaim openly? or thou again, why dost thou
inquire? for not only dost thou roundly blame, and grumble like a fool f. 54 b
(S. not a widow), and thou also givest forth curses like the heathen. Or hast
thou not heard what the Scripture saith, "Everyone who blesseth shall be Gen. xxvii. 29 *sic*
blessed, and every one who curseth shall be cursed"? Again in the Gospel Matt. v. 44
He said, "Bless them that curse you," and again He said, "When ye go into Luke x. 5
an house, say, Peace be to this house. And if the house be worthy of your Matt. x. 13
peace, it shall come upon it, but if it be not worthy, it shall return to you."
If therefore peace return to those that have sent it, more therefore shall Ap. Con. III. xv.
the curse be upon him who hath launched it. For if we (S. they) who have sent it out in vain, because he against whom it was sent was not worthy to receive a curse, everyone who curseth anyone in vain curseth
himself; for it is written in the Proverbs, "As the swallows and the birds Prov. xxvi. 2
fly, thus vain curses return." And again he said, that "those who send Prov. x. 18
forth curses are void of understanding"; for we are compared to the likeness
of the bee, as the Lord said, Go to the bee, and learn from her how Prov. vi. 6
she worketh, that she doeth her work with wisdom, and from her work food 8
is offered to the rich and the poor, for she is graceful and glorious, though

she hath little strength. Therefore as the bee with little strength, when she stingeth anyone leaveth her dart, is sterile and soon dieth, thus also we believers in this likeness, every evil thing that we do to another person we
Tobit iv. 15 are hurting ourselves. For everything that thou wouldst hate to happen
Gen. xxvii. 29 *sic* to thee, do not thou to another. Therefore everyone who blesseth is
f. 55 a blessed, and he who curseth is cursed. Admonish and reprove those who are without discipline. Admonish therefore, strengthen and increase those who act honestly. Let the widows therefore be removed from curses, for they are appointed to bless. Therefore neither let Bishop, nor Elder, nor Deacon, nor Widow send out a curse from their mouth, that they inherit not a curse, but a blessing. Let this be a care to thee, O Bishop, that not even one of the laity should send out a curse from his mouth; for thou hast the care of every man.

CHAPTER XVI.

Of the appointment of Deacons and Deaconesses, and of how it is fitting for them to conduct themselves in their service, without indolence of the mind nor license.

Therefore, O Bishop, appoint for thyself workers of righteousness and helpers, to help with thee to life, electing those who please thee from all the people (S. and appoint Deacons). The man who is elected is for many oversights that are required, but a woman for the service of the women; for there are houses where thou canst not send a Deacon to the women on account of the heathen. Send a Deaconess for many things. The office of a woman Deaconess is required, first, when women go down to the water, it is necessary that they be anointed by a Deaconess, and it is not fitting that the anointing oil should be given to a woman to touch; but rather the Deaconess. For it is necessary for the Priest who baptizeth, to anoint her who is baptized; but when there is a woman, and especially a Deaconess, it is not fitting for the women that they be seen by the men, but that by the laying on of the hand the head alone be
f. 55 b anointed, as of old time the Priests and Kings of Israel were anointed.
Ap. Con. III. xvi. Thou also, in like manner, by laying on [thy] hand, anoint the head of those who receive baptism, whether of men or of women, and afterwards, whether thou thyself baptize, or command the Deacon or the Elder to baptize, let it be a Deaconess, as we said before, who anoints the women. Let a man repeat over them the names of the invocation of the Godhead in the water. And when she that is baptized arises from the water let the Deaconess receive her, and teach her and educate her, in order that

the unbreakable seal of baptism be with purity and holiness. Therefore we affirm that the service of a woman, a Deaconess, is necessary and obligatory, because even our Lord and Saviour was served by the hand of women deaconesses, who were Mary the Magdalene, and Mary (Cod. S. daughter) of James, the mother of Joses, and the mother of Zebedee's children, with other women. This service of Deaconesses is necessary also to thee for many things, for in the houses of the heathen, where there are believing women, a Deaconess is required, that she may go in and visit those who are sick, and serve them with whatever they need, and anoint (S. wash) those who are healed from sicknesses.

Cod. S. *About Deacons.* Let the Deacons in their conduct resemble the Bishop; let them however work very much more than he. Let them not love filthy lucre, but let them be diligent in service. According to the number of the congregation of the Church let there be Deacons, that they may be able to distinguish and to comfort every one, so that to the aged women who have no strength, and to the brothers and sisters who are in sicknesses, they may prepare for every one of them the service that is fitting for him. But let a woman preferably be diligent in the service of the women, and a man, a Deacon, in the service of the men. Let him be ready to hear and to obey the command of the Bishop. In every place to which he is sent to serve or to say something to any one, let him work and labour; for it is necessary that every one should know his office, and be diligent in fulfilling it; and be of one counsel, and of one mind, and of one soul dwelling in two bodies. Know what that service is, as our Lord and Saviour said in the Gospel, "Whosoever among you wishes to be chief let him be your servant; even as the Son of Man came not to be ministered unto, but to minister, and to give His soul a ransom for many." Thus ye ought to work also, ye Deacons, even if ye have to give your lives for your brethren, in the service that is required of you. For even our Lord and Master did not despise when He served us, as it is written in Isaiah, "To justify the righteous who doeth a good service to many." If therefore the Lord of Heaven and of earth did service to us, bore and endured everything on our account, how much more is it required of us, that we should do thus to the brethren, that we, who are His imitators, and take the place of the Christ, should be like Him? You will find also that it is written in the Gospel, how our Lord girt a towel about His loins, and poured water into the wash-bason, while we were reclining, and drew near and washed the feet of us all, and dried [them] with the towel; but He did this, that He might show us the love and affection of brethren, that we also should do likewise to one another. If therefore our Lord did thus, ye Deacons, do ye hesitate to do thus to those who are sick and have no strength, ye who are doers of the Truth, and preserve the likeness of the Christ? Therefore serve in love, and do not grumble nor hesitate; but if not, if ye have done this service for the sake of men, and not for God, ye shall receive your reward according to your service in the day of judgment. It is therefore required of you Deacons, that ye visit all those who are in want, and make known to the Bishop those who are afflicted, that ye be his soul and his mind, and that ye labour and obey him in everything.

Ap. Con. III. xix.

Matt. xx. 27

Is. liii. 11

Cf. John xiii. 4, 5

CHAPTER XVII.

It is right that the Bishop should take care of orphans, those who are left young, and give them to be reared; and there is a condemnation on you, on those who have aught, and are not in want, who are greedy, and take of the gifts that are given to the Church for the orphans and the poor.

Ap. Con. IV. i. f. 56 a If one of the children of Christians be an orphan, either a boy or a girl, it is good that if there be one of the brethren who hath no children, he take the boy in place of children, and let him take a girl, every one who has a son; when her time comes let him give her to him in marriage, and fulfil his work in the service of God. If there be people who do not wish because of their riches[1] to do thus to orphan members, such people will meet also with the same, and they shall spend (S. their) parsimony in these Cf. Is. i. 7 things, and what the saints have not eaten, the Assyrians shall eat; and Ap. Con. IV. ii. strangers shall devour your land before your eyes. Ye therefore, O Bishops, take up the burden of them, that they be brought up so that nothing be wanting to them, and when it is the time for the maiden, give her in marriage to one of the brethren. And let the boy when he is grown up learn a handicraft, and when he is a man let him take the wage that is meet for his craft, (S. + and acquire the necessary tools,) that he may no longer be a burden on the charity of the brethren, which they had without deceit and without hypocrisy. And truly blessed is he who is able to help himself, and does not straiten the place of the orphans and the widows and the poor.

Ap. Con. IV. iii. *Those are guilty who take alms when they are not in want.* Woe unto them who possess, and who receive falsely. For every one of those who receives will give account to the Lord God in the day of judgment, of how he received, whether it was on account of childish orphanhood, or on account of the feebleness of old age, or on account of the weakness of sickness, or for the education of children that he received. Verily this man is also to be praised, he is considered as the Altar of God, therefore he shall be honoured by God; for it was not in vain that he received, for he prayed diligently at all times without idleness for those who gave. f. 56 b He offered his prayer, which is his strength, in return for his receiving, for such people shall receive from God a blessing in everlasting life. But

[1] S. + because of pleasing men, and being ashamed

those who possess, and receive by improbity[1], or again, who are idle, and instead of working and giving to others, themselves receive a gift, what therefore they have received shall be required of them, because they have straitened the place of the believing poor. Every one who has property Ap. Con. IV. iv.
and does not give to others, nor make use of it himself, lays up for himself a treasure which perishes on the earth; and inherits the place of the serpent who sits upon the treasure, and incurs the danger of being reckoned with it. For he who possesses, and receives by falsehood, does not believe in God, but in the mammon of iniquity, and because of the gains of avarice holds the Word in hypocrisy, and is filled with infidelity. He that is such, incurs the danger of being reckoned with the Infidels. But he who simply gives to every one, does well to give, and he is also pure who has received through necessity, and uses with sense what he has received; he has well received, and will be glorified by God in everlasting life and rest.

CHAPTER XVIII.

Exhortation to Bishops, that they watchfully take care not to receive gifts from those who are guilty, as for the provision of orphans and widows and the poor, not even if they are constrained to be degraded by hunger, and that they are guilty if they accept; and that the prayers of the poor are not heard when they pray for them that are such, being supplied by their goods. It is f. 57 a
fitting that they receive from the believing and the honest for the provision of the poor, and for the redemption of prisoners and the oppressed.

Therefore, O Bishops and Deacons, be constant in the service of Christ's Ap. Con. IV. vi.
Altar. For we have said about widows and orphans, that with all care and diligence ye shall observe the things that are given, what is the conduct of him or of her who gives for the provision, we say also again, of the Altar; because when widows are provided for by the work[2] of righteousness, they bring a holy and acceptable service before the Lord (S. + God Almighty) by means of His beloved Son and His holy Spirit, to Whom be glory and honour to all eternity. Amen. Therefore take care and be diligent that ye serve the widows with the service of a pure mind, that what they ask for be given [to them] quickly with their prayers. If there be any Bishops who are contemptuous, and pay no attention to these things through partiality, or for the sake of filthy lucre, or because they are careless and do not investigate, they shall give an account in no

[1] S. hypocrisy

[2] S. people

ordinary manner. For they accept what is for the service of the provision for orphans and widows, from the rich who have put people in prison, who act badly towards their servants, or who deal hardly in their cities, or who oppress the poor, or from the impure and from those who use their bodies wickedly (S. C. + or from doers of evil), from those who diminish and lend with usury; (S. C. + or from villainous advocates); (S. + or from infamous accusers); or from judges who are accepters of persons; (S. C. + or from the concocters of poisons; or from the makers of idols); from worshippers of gold or silver or brass (S. C. + as thieves; or from unjust publicans; or from seers of visions); from those who change weights, or
f. 57 b from those who measure in deceit; or from tavern-keepers who mix [wine] with water; or from soldiers who conduct themselves iniquitously; (S. C. + or from murderers; or from guilty executioners); or from any arrogant princes who have been polluted in wars, and have shed innocent blood unjustly; (S. C. + or from the reversers of judgments who for theft act unjustly and deceitfully towards the country people and all the poor; and from worshippers of idols; or from the polluted); or from the usurers and the covetous; those therefore that from these [persons] provide for widows and the poor, will be found guilty in the judgment of the (S. C. + day of
Prov. xv. 17 the) Lord; because the Lord[1] hath said, "Better is a dinner of herbs with love and peace than a slaughter of fatted oxen with hatred." If a widow be nourished only with food from honest work, it will be of profit to her; but if aught be given to her from abundance of iniquity, it will be a certain loss to her. If a widow be nourished by aught that is unjust, she cannot offer her service and her prayer (S. C. + in innocence) before God; even if she be just who prays for the wicked, her prayer for them will not be heard, but only [that] for herself; for God is a trier of hearts and He receives prayers in righteousness (S. C. + and discrimination), but if they pray for those who have sinned and repent, their prayers will also be heard; for those who are enchained in sins and do not repent, not only are they certainly unheard when they pray, but they also call their delinquencies to mind before God.

Those Bishops are culpable who take alms from the guilty. Therefore,
Deut. xxiii. 18 O Bishops, flee from such services; for it is written, "Thou shalt not take up to the altar of the Lord the price of a dog nor the wages of a harlot." For if the widows in their blindness pray for adulterers and transgressors of the law, [2]their prayers are not heard[2]. Ye cause a blasphemy to come upon the Word by your evil administration, as if there were not a good and

[1] S. C. Scripture

[2] S. C. they are not heard, not receiving their requests

liberal God. Be very watchful therefore that ye serve not the Altar of God f. 58 a
from the services of a transgressor, for there is no cause for your saying,
We did not know, for ye have heard what the Scripture has said, "Remove Is. liv. 14
from evil, and fear not" (S. B. C. + and terror shall not come near thee). Ap. Con. IV. viii.
Say not, These are they who alone give alms, and if we do not accept from them, from whence shall the orphans and widows who are in straits be served? God has said to you [1]not to take from the wicked and help the Churches[1], it were profitable for you to be tortured by hunger, rather than to take from the wicked. Therefore investigate and prove, that ye may receive from believers, those who are in communion with the Church[2] and conduct themselves aright, that ye may nourish those who are in straits. Do not receive from those who are put out of the Church and are blameable, until they are thought worthy to become members of the Church. But if ye be in want, tell the brethren, let them work amongst you, and
give; serve thus with justice. Teach and say to the people, that it is Ap. Con. IV. ix.
written, "Honour the Lord with honest work, and with the first of all thy Prov. iii. 9
fruits." Therefore with the honest work of believers nourish and clothe those who are greatly in want (S. C. + and what is given to you by them, as we said to you before, distribute it at the time for the ransom of believers). Ransom slaves and captives, and those who are treated with violence, those who are condemned [3]by the mob[3], (S. + those who are condemned to the circus, or to the mines, or to exile, or to the amphitheatre), and those who are in straits (S. C. + Let the Deacons go in to them), let them visit every
one and provide them with what they are in want of. If it should happen Ap. Con. IV. x.
that ye take from the wicked, against your will, make no use of it for nourishment, unless it be just a little, expend it in wood [4]for fire[4]; lest a widow being in straits should buy with it some food for herself. Thus let
the widows, not being polluted by evil, pray that they may receive from f. 58 b
God all good things that they ask and seek. Also each one of them by herself, and ye also, will not be held by these sins.

[1] S. B. C. Because ye have received the gifts of the Levites, the firstfruits and offerings of your people, that ye may be nourished, and have also a superfluity that ye be not straitened and take from the wicked. But if the Churches are so poor, that those who are in want must be nourished by such people

[2] S. Churches

[3] S. unlawfully by the crowd

[4] S. C. for yourselves and for the widows

CHAPTER XIX.

Exhortation to Bishops to take care of those who are persecuted or imprisoned for the name of the Christ, that they visit them, and keep away from him who is imprisoned and receives punishment from judges because of his depravity. Also exhortation to all Christians that they suffer with those who suffer for the sake of the Christ, and that out of fear they deny not or forsake them. He who denieth them, denieth Christianity and the Christ. And let him pray that he enter not into temptation.

Ap. Con. V. i. Do not take your eyes off the Christian who is put in prison for the name of God, and for his faith and love, and [1]is cast into the mines[1]; but by your work and by the sweat of your face send him nourishment, and for the wage of the soldiers who guard him, that he may be at ease and be taken care of, but that your blessed brother be not completely afflicted. For he who is condemned for the name of God the Christ, let him be considered by you as a holy Martyr, and an Angel of God, (S. + or as God upon earth) he who is clothed spiritually with the Holy Ghost (S. + of God, by whose means ye behold the Lord our Saviour), because he has been thought worthy of an incorruptible crown (S. + he has renewed the testimony of the Passion). Therefore it is obligatory that all ye believers should diligently comfort the Martyrs with your goods (S. + by means of your Bishops). But if there be a man who has nothing, let him fast, and what he would have spent for himself for that day, let him give to his brother. But if thou art rich, it is required of thee that thou serve them according to thy power, or even that thou give all thy property to redeem them from the chains [2]of death[2], for they
f. 59a are worthy of God, and children who fulfil His will, as the Lord hath
Matt. x. 32 said, "Whosoever shall confess Me before men, him will I also confess before My Father which is in heaven." Do not be ashamed [3]to talk with[3] them when they[4] are imprisoned, and in doing these things ye shall inherit everlasting life, for ye shall be partakers in their martyrdom; as we know
Matt. xxv. 34 that our Lord hath spoken thus in the Gospel, "Come unto Me, all ye
blessed of My Father, inherit the kingdom that is prepared for you before
35 the foundation of the world. I was hungry, and ye fed Me; I was thirsty,
36 and ye gave Me drink; I was a stranger, and ye gathered Me in; I was
37 naked, and ye clothed Me; in prison, and ye came unto Me. Then shall

[1] S. is condemned to the amphitheatre, or to the beasts, or to the mines

[2] S. om. [3] S. to visit [4] Cod. ye

the righteous answer and say, 'Lord, when saw we Thee hungry, and fed
Thee; or thirsty, and gave Thee to drink; or naked, and we clothed 38 *sic*
Thee; or sick, and we visited Thee; or a stranger, and we gathered 39 *sic*
Thee in; or in prison, and we came unto Thee?' And he shall answer 40
and say unto them, 'that all that ye have done to My little brethren,
ye have done it unto Me.' Then shall the righteous go unto eternal life." 46
But if there be a man who is called a Christian, and he should stumble, Ap. Con. V. ii.
and be tempted by Satan, and be reproved for wicked works, either theft
or murder, keep away from any that are such; lest one of you be tempted
by those who belong to him. For if a heathen should lay hold of thee, and
ask thee and say to thee; Thou art also a Christian like that man, thou
canst not deny that thou art a Christian, but thou confessest, and thou
art not condemned as a Christian, but art punished as an evil-doer, for
thou wast asked if thou wert like that man, and thy confession is in vain
to thee; if thou deniest, thou hast denied the Lord. Therefore keep
away from them, that ye may be without offence. But help with much
zeal those believers, your members, who are in the bond of iniquity as
evil-doers and are imprisoned, and free them from the hand of the wicked[1]. f. 59 b
For if some one approach those who are imprisoned for the name of
the Christ our Lord, and is laid hold of along with them, blessed shall
he be that he has been thought worthy of all this companionship.
Receive and refresh those who are persecuted on account of the Faith, Ap. Con. V. iii.
who migrate from city to city according to the Lord's command, rejoicing
that ye are partakers of their persecution; for our Lord spake about
you in the Gospel, "Blessed are ye when they persecute you, and upbraid Matt. v. 11
you for My name"; because when a Christian is persecuted, and killed
because of the Faith, [2]he is a Martyr of God[2]; (S. + and henceforth he will
not be persecuted by any one, for he is known of the Lord). But if he deny Ap. Con. V. iv.
that he is a Christian, he will be called a [cause of] offence; he will not[3]
be persecuted by men, but he will be rejected by God because of his
denials (S. + and henceforth he will have no part with the saints in the
everlasting kingdom, and according to the promise of the Lord; but
his inheritance shall be with the wicked), for the Lord God hath said,
"Whosoever denieth Me, or is ashamed of Me and of My words, I Matt. x. 33 *sic*
will deny him before My Father which is in heaven, when I come
(S. + with strength and glory) to judge the quick and the dead." Again
it is written, "Every one who loveth his father and mother more than 37

[1] S. + But if any one joins himself to them, and is taken along with them, and is confined, being innocent, for the sake of his brother; blessed is he that he is called a Christian, that he has acknowledged the Lord, and that he will live before Him

[2] S. he becomes a man of God

[3] S. om. not

Me, is not worthy of Me (S. + and every one who loveth his son or
38 *sic* his daughter more than Me is not worthy of Me); and every one who
taketh not up his cross, rejoicing, and cometh not after Me, is not worthy
of Me." (S. + and "every one who loseth his life because of Me shall
Mark viii. 36 find it, and every one that saveth his life by denying shall lose it.) For
37 what shall it profit a man, if he gain the whole world, and lose his soul,
Matt. x. 28 *sic* or what shall a man give in exchange for his soul?"; and again, "Fear
not those who kill the body, but they cannot kill the soul; rather fear
Ap. Con. V. v. Me, who am able to destroy soul and body in hell." Now every one
who learns a handicraft looks at his master, and sees how by means of his
craft and knowledge he perfects his work; he also imitates him, and
perfects the work that has been entrusted to him that he may not hear
upbraiding from him, but if he come short of what has been entrusted
f. 60 a to him, he is [1]not a disciple[1]; but we who have a master and teacher,
[2]our Lord and Saviour, who rose incorruptible from the grave, because
by His doctrine we possess incorruptible beauty[2], thus He came in poverty;
He also separated Himself from Mary, His blessed mother, and from His
brethren, also from Himself, and endured persecution even unto the Cross.
These things He suffered on our account, that He might save us who believe,
who are of the house of Israel[3], from chains and condemnations, which we
have mentioned before, and deliver you who are of the Gentiles from the
worship of idols and from all iniquity. If therefore the Christ suffered on
our account, to save us who believe in Him, why should we not resemble
Him in His sufferings when He has given us patience? and these things
[are] for our own sake, that we may be delivered from the Gehenna[4] of fire.
For He suffered for us; let us suffer for ourselves (S. + or does our
Lord certainly need that we should suffer for Him except for this only
that He would prove the warmth of our faith and the desire of our souls?).
Ap. Con. V. vi. Let us separate ourselves from our fathers and from our tribe, and from
all that is in the world, and turn from ourselves, praying that we fall not
into temptation. But if we are called to martyrdom, being questioned, let
us confess; suffering, let us endure; being oppressed, let us rejoice; being
persecuted, let us not be saddened; because it is not only our own souls
that we are delivering (S. + from hell, by acting thus), but also those who
are children in the faith, (S. + and we teach the hearers to act thus,) that
they may live before God. But if we are defaulters towards the faith
in the Lord, and deny because of the weakness of the flesh, as the Lord

[1] S. not perfect

[2] S. why do we not resemble Him in His doctrine and conduct, because He forsook riches and beauty and power and glory

[3] I accept Dr Nestle's emendation, that ܐܢ̈ܫܐ is a scribe's error for ܐܝܣܪܝܠ

[4] S. death

hath said, "The spirit is ready and willing, but the flesh is weak," it Matt. xxvi. 41
is not merely ourselves whom we destroy, but also the souls of our brethren (S. + we kill along with ourselves); for when they see our denials, they will think that they have been taught [1]error of doctrines[1], and when they are [2]made captive[2] we shall have to answer for them as well as for ourselves, every one of us to the Lord in the day of judgment. (S. + But if thou art taken and brought before the governor, and deniest thy hope in the Lord in thy holy faith, and art set free to-day, but to-morrow thou art sick with a fever, and fallest on thy bed, or thy stomach pain thee, and thou takest no food, but givest it back with severe pains, or fallest into the affliction of gripes, or of the hurt of one of thy members; or thou sendest forth from thy bowels blood and gall by severe pains; or thou hast a tumour in one of thy members; and thou art cut up by the hands of doctors, and diest in afflictions and in great agonies, what will thy denial that thou hast made profit thee, O man? for behold, thou hast caused thy soul to inherit pains and sufferings, and thou hast lost thy eternal life before God. Thou wilt burn and be tormented without rest
for ever; as the Lord hath said, "Every one who loveth his life shall lose John xii. 25 *sic*
it; and every one that loseth his life for My sake shall find it." Therefore the Christian who denies, loves his life for a short time in this world, that he may not die for the sake of the name of the Lord God; but he destroys himself for ever in the fire, for he himself falls into hell,
because Christ denies him, as He hath said in the Gospel, "Whoso- Matt. x. 33
ever denieth Me before men, I also will deny him before my Father
which is in Heaven." But those whom the Lord denieth go out and Matt. viii. 12
are cast into outer darkness, and there they shall have weeping and gnashing of teeth; for He has said that "every one who loveth his life more than Me is not worthy of Me.") But let us be diligent, my brethren,
to commend our lives to the Lord God; and if a man be found worthy f. 60 b
of martyrdom, let him receive it with joy, that he is thought worthy of this crown, and that his exit from this world should be by martyrdom; for our
Saviour has said that "there is no disciple that is above his Lord, but let Luke vi. 40
every one be perfect like his Lord." (S. + Our Lord therefore chose all these sufferings in order to save us; He accepted to be beaten and blasphemed against, and His face spat upon, and to drink vinegar and myrrh, and at length He endured even to being hanged upon the cross.) We therefore who are His disciples, let us be imitators of Him; for if He endured everything for our sakes (S. even to sufferings) how much ought not we to bear for

[1] S. doctrines of error [2] S. scandalized

ourselves? suffering and not hesitating, for thus He has counselled us, that if even we were to burn in coals of fire, let us believe in the Lord Jesus the Christ, and in His Father, the Lord God Almighty, and in the Holy Ghost, to whom be glory and honour for ever and ever. Amen.

CHAPTER XX.

About the Resurrection of the dead, we are taught not only by the Holy Scriptures, but also by means of demonstrations from the books of the heathen; and by means also of these natural demonstrations let us, being diligent, like believing men who have a sure hope of the Resurrection, not excuse ourselves from martyrdom on account of the Christ, if we are called to it.

Ap. Con. V. vii. God the Father Almighty will raise us by means of God our
Saviour, as He has promised. He will raise us from among the dead
just as we are, in the likeness in which we now are; nevertheless there
shall not be wanting to us the great glory of everlasting life; for even
should we be thrown into the depths of the sea, or scattered by the
winds like chaff, we shall always be within this world, and all this
world is enclosed in the hand of God, and therefore from the interior
Luke xxi. 18 of His hand the Lord God will raise us, as He[1] hath said, "A hair
19 of your head shall not perish," and "in your patience possess ye your
souls." About the resurrection and about the glory of martyrs the Lord
Daniel xii. 2 hath said in Daniel thus, that "many who sleep in the surface of the earth
f. 61 a shall arise in that day, some to everlasting life, and some to shame
3 *sic* and contempt (S. + and dispersion). And they that be wise shall shine
as the lights of heaven, and those that are mighty in the Word as the
stars of heaven." As the sun and as the moon (S. + those lights of
heaven), He hath promised to give (S. + the glorious light) to those
who (S. + are wise, and) are martyrs for his Name. And it is not to
believers[2] that He hath promised resurrection, but also to all men; for
Ezek. xxxvii. 1 He hath said thus in Ezekiel, "The hand of the Lord was upon me,
and he led me out into (S. in the Spirit and set me in the midst of)
2 the plain, and it was full of bones, and He caused me to pass by
them round about, etc. (S. + and they were many and very dry.
3 And He said unto me, Son of man, do these bones live? And I said,
4 Thou knowest, O Lord God. And the Lord said unto me, Prophesy
upon these bones, and say unto them, O ye dry bones, hear ye the word
5 of the Lord. Thus saith the Lord God unto these bones, Behold, I will

[1] S. the Lord and Saviour

[2] S. martyrs only

cause breath to enter into you, and ye shall live; I will put sinews 6
upon you, and build flesh upon you, and clothe you with skin, and I
will give breath into you, and ye shall live, and ye shall know that
I am the Lord. So I prophesied as He had said to me, and as I 7
prophesied there was a voice, and a shaking, and the bones came together, bone to bone; and I saw that sinews and flesh came up upon 8
them, and skin was drawn over them from above, but there was no
breath in them. And the Lord said unto me, Prophesy unto the wind, 9
and say, Thus saith the Lord God, Come, O wind, from the four
quarters, and enter into these dead men, and they shall live. So I pro- 10
phesied as He commanded me, and the wind came into them, and they
lived; and they stood up upon their feet, in a great army. And 11
the Lord said unto me, Son of man, those bones are they of the house
of Israel, who say, Our bones are dried, and our hope is destroyed,
and we are not. Thus saith the Lord God, Behold, I open your graves, 12
and I will bring you from thence, O my people, and I will lead you
into the land of Israel; and ye shall know that I am the Lord when 13
I open your graves, to bring out My people from the tombs. And I will 14
put My Spirit into you, and ye shall live, and I shall cause you to dwell
in your land, and ye shall know that I am the Lord who hath spoken
and done, and all the dwellers on earth shall be at peace, saith the
Lord."

Again He hath said by means of Isaiah, "All they that sleep and Is. xxvi. 19
the dead shall arise, and all that are in the graves shall awake, for thy
dew is unto them the dew of healing, but the land of the wicked shall be
destroyed.")

And again he hath spoken by means of Isaiah [1]the prophet[1] about the Resurrection and eternal life and about the glory of the righteous, and also about the shame and destruction of sinners, (S. + about their conduct, and their fall, about their dissolution, their ruin, and their condemnation, for when He said that the land of the wicked shall fall, he spoke of their body, because it is from the earth, and will be accounted with shame as of the earth; because they did not worship God, they shall fall into fire and torment). And in the Twelve Prophets they said
thus, "Behold, ye wicked, and see and understand wonders, and return Habakkuk i. 5
to corruption, for I will work a work in your days (S. + which if a man
declare it unto you ye will not believe.") These things and more than these are said against those who do not believe in the Resurrection, and

[1] S. and all the other prophets

against those who deny God, (S. + and against those who do not worship God, and against transgressors of the Law and against the heathen,) that when they shall see the glory of believers they shall return to perish in the fire because they did not believe. But we have learnt and believed in His Resurrection from the dead. The Resurrection which God has promised to us is sure to us and not deceptive, because our Saviour Himself is the earnest of our resurrection, He having risen first.

Confirmation about the Resurrection, even from the writings of the heathen. Also those among the Gentiles who read, read and hear, even among the heathen, about the Resurrection from the Sybil, what was said and
Oracula Sybillina c. iv. 179—185 (ed. Rzach) preached to them thus, "When everything shall be dust and ashes, the Most High God shall cause the fire which He hath kindled to cease, and then God Himself shall raise the bones and ashes of men, and shall
f. 61 b clothe them with their likeness, and raise men as they were before. And then the judgment shall take place, in which God shall judge the wicked
187—190 in the future world, and the earth shall cover the impious. The just and the righteous shall live in the land of life; God will give them spirit and goodness, (S. + and life) and thereafter they shall all see one another." It is not only, my friends, by means of the Sybil that the Resurrection was preached to the heathen, but also by means of the holy Scriptures, before the Lord preached to the Jews and to the heathen and to the Christians together, and announced the Resurrection of the dead which shall come to men.

(S. + *Confirmation about the Resurrection also from natural demonstrations.*) God shows us abundantly about the Resurrection, even by means of a bird that cannot speak, we mean the phœnix, which is solitary, for if it had a mate many would be seen by man, but now one alone is seen once in five hundred years, which enters Egypt and goes to the altar that is called of the Sun. It brings cinnamon; as it prays towards the East, the fire kindles of itself, and consumes it, so that it becomes ashes; and again from the ashes is formed a worm, which grows up in its likeness, and becomes a perfect phœnix, and thereafter it departs and goes whence it came.)

Confirmation that we must not excuse ourselves from Martyrdom for the sake of the Christ. If therefore God has shown us about the Resurrection by means of an irrational animal, much more we who believe in the Resurrection of God and in the promise of God, if martyrdom come upon us as on men worthy of all this glory of God, shall receive the incorruptible crown in eternal life, and in the glorious honour of the martyrdom of God;

let us receive it joyfully with all our hearts, and let us believe in the Lord God who will raise us in glorious light. As in the beginning, God commanded by a word, (S. + and the world was) and He said, Let there be light, and night and day; and heaven and earth and seas, and birds and beasts, and creeping things of the earth (S. + and fourfooted beasts) and trees, and everything was established (S. +in its nature) by His Word, as the Scripture hath said, (S. + all these works that were done were by means of the obedience they give Him; they witness about God who made them, that "He created and founded them out of nothing," (S. + they also show a sign of the Resurrection. As therefore He made everything,) thus also man who is His creature He will especially vivify and raise (S. + For if He founded and established the world out of nothing, this would be still more easy, that out of nothing He should vivify and raise man, who is the creature of His hands), and as with human seed He clothes man with a garment in the womb and makes him grow. If therefore He shall raise all men, as He hath said in Isaiah, "All flesh shall see the salvation of God," Is. lii. 10
yet more will He vivify and raise believers (S. + and again the believers of believers, who are the Martyrs, He will vivify and raise and establish in great glory, and make them His councillors), because to the simple disciples who believe in Him, He hath promised a glory like that of the stars; but (S. + to the Martyrs) He hath promised to give eternal f. 62 a
glory, (S. + like shining bodies that are not wearied with exceeding light, which shine continually. Therefore, as disciples of the Christ, let us believe that we shall receive from Him all good things which He hath counselled and promised us in eternal life. Let us be conformed to all His doctrine and to His patience.) Let us believe in His birth from a virgin, and in His coming and in His willing Passion. Let us be convinced by means of the Holy Scriptures, as the Prophets announced beforehand everything about His coming, and (S. + all these things) were confirmed in our hearts (S. + for even the demons, when they trembled at His name, extolled His coming. You believe therefore and are convinced of the things that we said before); and we still more, we who were with Him, and saw Him with our eyes and ate with Him, and were companions and witnesses of His coming, we believe in the great unspeakable things (S. gifts) which He will give as He hath promised. (S. + Let us believe and hope that we shall receive, for all our faith is surely proved) if we believe in His promises that they shall be. Let us be called to martyrdom for His name's sake; when we go out of this world by confession, we Ap. Con. V. viii.
are sanctified from all our sins (S. + and follies, and we shall be found

Psalm xxxii. 1, 2 pure, for He hath said in David about martyrs thus, "Blessed are they
whose transgression is forgiven, and whose sins are covered. Blessed
is the man to whom the Lord will not impute his sins." Therefore the
Martyrs are blessed and pure from all follies, who are raised above all
evil and taken away from it, as He said in Isaiah about the Christ and His
Is. lvii. 1 Martyrs, "Behold, the righteous perisheth, and no man considereth; and
holy men are taken away, and no one careth for it; for the righteous is
2 gathered away before the evil, and his grave shall be in peace." But these
things are said about those who suffer martyrdom for the name of the
Christ. Sins are also forgiven) in baptism to those who come from the
heathen and enter the holy Church of God. (S. + Let us ask again
to whom sins are not imputed.) Their sins are considered like Abraham
and Isaac and Jacob (S. + and all the Patriarchs, as well as the Martyrs.
Prov. xx. 6 Hear then, my brethren) for the Scripture saith, "Who shall boast himself
and say, I am pure from sins, or who will (S. + dare to) say, I am holy?"
Job xiv. 4, 5 and again, "There is no man clean from pollution, even if his life should
be only for a day upon the earth." Every one therefore who believeth
and is baptized, his former sins are forgiven; but should he again sin
after baptism, (S. + even if he do not commit a mortal sin or participate
in it, but only seeth or heareth or speaketh, and thus again) he is guilty
of the sin. If then one go out of this world by martyrdom for the name
of the Lord, blessed is he; for the brethren who have suffered martyrdom
and have gone out of this world, in these things their sins are covered
(S. + Behold, like this, that "every one who looketh on a woman to lust
after her," hear also, "accusation and evil speaking," or like this, that
"every vain word that men shall speak," etc.)

CHAPTER XXI.

Exhorting every Christian to keep himself from all evil and frivolous conversation, and from all bad and heathenish conduct. About the Holy f. 62 b *Fast. About the Passion and Crucifixion of our Lord. About the fourteenth [day] of the Passover of the Jews; about the Friday of the Passion, and the Sabbath of the Annunciation and the Sunday of the Resurrection of our Saviour. About the mourning of the Sabbath-day of the nation of the Jews, and about the rejoicing of the people of the Christians.*

Ap. Con. V. x. Therefore it is required of the Christian that he keep himself from vain work, and from lascivious and impure words, (S. + even on Sundays when we are glad and rejoice) no one is allowed to say a word

that belongs to sport or is foreign to the fear of God. (S. + as our
Lord also taught us in the Psalm, in David, and saith thus, "Now there- Ps. ii. 10
fore understand, ye kings, and be instructed, all ye judges of the earth;
serve the Lord with fear, and rejoice before Him with trembling. Attend 11, 12
to discipline, lest the Lord be angry, and ye perish from the way of justice,
because His anger is kindled but a little against you; blessed are all
they that put their trust in Him.") But it is therefore required of us that
we keep feasts, and that we make our rejoicing with fear and trembling,
for a believing Christian ought not to recite the hymns of the heathen, Ap. Con. V. xi.
nor to approach those foreign customs, [1]nor to[1] remember the name of
an idol, may this be far from believers! for the Lord rebuketh in Jeremiah
and saith, "They have forsaken Me, and sworn by those that are not gods," Jer. v. 7
(S. + and again He saith, "If Israel will return unto Me, let him return, Jer. iv. 1
saith the Lord, and if he will take away his abominations from his mouth,
and will fear before My face, and will swear as the Lord liveth," and 2
again He saith, "I will take the name of the idols from your mouth." By Zech. xiii. 2 *sic*
means of Moses again He saith to them, "They have moved Me to jealousy Deut. xxxii. 21
with that which is no God, and with their idols they have made Me angry."
And in all the Scriptures He speaketh against these things, and not only
concerning the idols.) It is not allowed to believers to swear, not by Ap. Con. V. xii.
the sun nor by the moon, for the Lord God hath spoken thus by means
of Moses, "My people, if ye see the sun and the moon, be not led astray Deut. iv. 19
by them, nor worship them; for the Lord hath given them to you for
lights upon the earth." (S. + and by means of Jeremiah again He saith,
"Learn not according to the ways of the heathen, and be not afraid of Jer. x. 2
the signs of heaven.") And by means of Ezekiel He hath said thus,
"And He brought me into the court of the house of the Lord, between the Ezek. viii. 16
porch and the altar, and I saw there men with their loins girt towards the
temple of the Lord, and their faces opposite the East, and they were
worshipping the sun. And the Lord said unto me, Son of man, is this a 17
small thing to the house of Judah to commit these abominations here? and
they have filled the land with iniquity. (S. + and they have returned to
provoke Me to anger, and they are as mockers. I also will deal in fury; 18
mine eye shall not spare, nor will I have pity; even if they cry in Mine
ears with a loud voice, I will not hear them." Ye see, beloved, how
severely and bitterly the Lord giveth judgment in His wrath against
those who worship the sun or swear by it.) It is therefore unlawful for the
believer to swear either by the sun or by any of the signs of heaven (S. + or

[1] S. and doctrines of assemblies, for it will happen that by means of hymns, he will

the elements); either to mention the name of an idol with his mouth, or to
let a curse go out of his mouth, but only blessings (S. + and psalms, and
the authoritative and divine Scriptures, which are the foundations of the
f. 63a truth of our faith), especially in the day of the fast and the holy Passover,
Ap. Con. V. xiii. in which all believers fast (S. + who are in all the world), as our Lord and
Mark ii. 19 Teacher said, when they asked Him, "Why do the disciples of John fast,
and Thy disciples fast not?" And He said unto them, "The children of the
bridechamber cannot fast while the bridegroom is with them, (S. + but the
days will come when the bridegroom shall be taken from them, and then
shall they fast in those days)." Now then by means of His deeds He is
with us (S. + but to sight He is far off, because He hath risen to the heights
of Heaven, and sitteth at the right hand of His Father). Therefore when
ye fast, pray and implore for those who are lost, as we also did when our
Ap. Con. V. xiv. Lord was suffering; for while He was yet with us before He suffered,
Cf. Matt. xxvi. 21 while we were eating the Passover with Him, He said to us, "This day,
in this night, one of you betrayeth Me." And every one of us said to Him,
22 "Surely it is not I, Lord?" And He answered and said unto us, "He who
23 stretcheth out his hand with Me in the dish." He signified Judas Iscariot,
John vi. 71 who was [1]one of the twelve[1]. (S. +[2] Then our Lord said unto us, "Verily
Cf. Matt. xxvi. 31 I say unto you, yet a little while, and ye shall leave Me, for it is written,
I will smite the shepherd, and the sheep of His flock shall be scattered."
And Judas came with the scribes and with the priests of the people, and
delivered up our Lord Jesus. But this was on Wednesday, for when we had
eaten the Passover on Tuesday in the evening, we went out to the Mount
of Olives, and in the night they took our Lord Jesus; and on the next
day, which was Wednesday, He remained in prison in the house of Cepha
the High Priest. In that day the chiefs of the people were assembled, and
they took counsel together against Him. Again, the next day, which was
Thursday, they brought Him to Pilate the governor, and again He remained
in prison with Pilate, in the night after Thursday. And when it dawned on
Friday, they accused Him much before Pilate, yet they could show nothing
true, but they brought false witness against Him. And they asked Him
from Pilate, to put Him to death, and they crucified Him on Friday. At
six o'clock therefore on Friday He suffered, and these hours during which
our Lord was crucified have been reckoned a day, afterwards it was again
dark for three hours, and it was reckoned a night; and again from the
ninth hour till the evening, three hours, a day; and again afterwards the
night of Passion Sabbath; but in the Gospel of Matthew it is thus written,

[1] S. one of us, who betrayed Him

[2] The addition in S. reaches to p. 97

that "[1]in the evening of the Sabbath, when the first day of the week
dawned[1], came Mary, and another Mary, the Magdalene, to see the Matt.
sepulchre. And there was a great earthquake, for the angel of the Lord xxviii.
came down and rolled the stone." And again the Sabbath-day. Then 2
three hours of the night after the Sabbath, in which our Lord slept [and
rose], and the saying was fulfilled (marg. Take heed!) that "it is required Matt. xii.
of the Son of Man that He should pass through the heart of the earth, 40
three days and three nights," as it is written in the Gospel. Again, it is
written in David, "Behold, thou hast appointed my days by measure," Ps. xxxix.
because therefore these days and nights are made shorter. Thus it is written, 5 *sic*
"In the night therefore, as the first day of the week dawned, He was seen Cf. Matt.
by Mary Magdalene, and by Mary the daughter of James; and in the xxviii. 1
night of the first day of the week He went in to Levi, and then He was
seen also by us." But He said unto us when He was teaching us, "Will ye Ap. Con.
fast because of Me in these days? or do I need that ye afflict yourselves? V. xv.
but for the sake of your brethren ye have done this, and do it in these days
when ye fast; and on Wednesday, and on Friday at all times, as it is
written in Zechariah, 'The fast of the fourth and the fast of the fifth,' Zech. viii.
which is Friday; for it is not lawful for you to fast on Sunday, because it 19
belongs to My resurrection; wherefore Sunday is not counted amongst the
numbers of the fast-days of the Passion, but they are counted from Monday,
and are five days. Therefore let the fourth fast, and the fifth fast, and the
seventh fast, and the tenth fast be to those of the house of Israel. Fast,
therefore, from Monday, fully six days, until the night after the Sabbath,
and let it be counted to you as a week; but the tenth, because the beginning
of My name is a *yod*[2], in which is the beginning of the fasts, but is not as a
feast of the former people, but as a new covenant which I have appointed
to you, that you should fast on their behalf on Wednesday, because on
Wednesday they began to destroy themselves and laid hold of Me; for the
night after Tuesday, which was Wednesday, as it is written, that 'the
evening and the morning were one day,' the evening [see that thou take Gen. i. 19
heed!] therefore belongs to the day that follows it, for on Tuesday in
the evening I ate with you My passover, and in the night they laid hold
on Me [fast then], but again also on Friday, fast on their behalf, because
on it they crucified Me in the midst of their feast of unleavened bread, as it
was foretold by David, 'In the midst of their feasts they have put their Ps. lxxiv. 4

[1] Cod. Brit. Mus. adds here "He rose; and again it was the Sabbath day, and then three hours of the night after the Sabbath, in which our Lord rose"

[2] The letter *yod*, being the tenth letter in the Hebrew and Syriac alphabets, serves also as a numeral signifying 10.

signs, and have not known.' But do ye fast constantly during these days
at all times, especially those who are from the Gentiles; for because the
nation doth not obey I have separated them from the blindness and from the
error of idols; and I have received them in order that by means of your
fast, and of those who are Gentiles, and your worship during those days,
whilst ye are praying and imploring on account of the error and ruin of
the nation, your prayer and entreaty may be accepted before My Father
which is in heaven, as from the one mouth of all the believers that are on
the earth, and all that they have done to Me may be forgiven them.
Therefore also in the Gospel I said before to you, 'Pray for your enemies';
and 'Blessed are they who mourn for the perdition of unbelievers.'"
Therefore know, brethren, that our fast which we keep in the Passover,
because our brethren have not obeyed, ye shall keep even if they hate you;
but brethren we are bound to call them, because it is written for us thus in
Isaiah lxvi. 5 Isaiah, "Call them brethren that hate you and reject you, that the name of
the Lord may be glorified." On account of them and of the judgment therefore and corruption of the land we are required to fast and mourn, that
we may rejoice and be glad in the world to come, as it is written in Isaiah,
Is. xii. 6 *sic* "Rejoice, all ye who mourn over Zion," and again He saith, "to comfort all
Is. lxi. 3 those who mourn over Zion; instead of ashes the oil of joy, and instead of the
spirit of heaviness the garment of glory." It is required of us therefore to
have pity upon them, and to believe, and to fast and pray for them; because
that when our Lord came to the nation they did not believe Him when
He was teaching them, but they let His teaching pass away from their
ears. Because therefore this nation obeyed not, He received you, brethren,
who are from the Gentiles, and He opened your ears for the hearing of
your heart, as our Lord and Saviour said by means of Isaiah the prophet,
Is. lxv. 1 "I was seen of those that asked not for Me; I was found of those that
sought Me not; and I have said, Behold Me, to a people who have not called
[upon] My name." About whom therefore did He thus speak? was it not
about the Gentiles, because they had never known God, and because they
had worshipped idols? but when our Lord came to the world and taught
you, ye believed, ye who believed in Him, that God is one. And again those
believe who are worthy, until the number of the saved shall be completed;
Ps. lxviii. 17 a thousand times a thousand and ten thousand times ten thousand, as it is
written in David; but about the nation which did not believe in Him thus
Is. lxv. 2 He said, "I have stretched out My hands all the day unto a people who
will not be persuaded and are disobedient, and who walk in a way that
3 is not good, and who go after their sins, a people who provoke Me to anger

before Me." See therefore that the people provoked our Lord to anger Ap. Con. V. xvi.
because they did not believe in Him; wherefore He saith that "they provoked Is. lxiii. 10
the Holy Spirit to anger, and turned themselves to enmity." And again
otherwise He saith about them by means of Isaiah the prophet, "The Is. ix. 1
land of Zebulun, the land of Naphtali, the way of the sea, beyond the
Jordan, Galilee of the nations; the people that sat [in] darkness, ye have 2
seen a great light, and those who sat in darkness and in the shadows of
death, upon them hath the light shined." "Those that sat in darkness," He said, about those from the Nation who believed in our Lord Jesus; for because of the blindness of the Nation a great darkness surrounded them; for they saw Jesus, and they did not know that He was the Christ, and did not understand Him, not from the writings of the Prophets, nor from His works and healings; but to you of the Nation who believe in Jesus we say, that ye have learnt how the Scripture testifieth about us and saith, "they have seen the great light." Ye therefore who have believed in Him, ye have seen a great Light, Jesus the Christ our Lord. And again those who believe in Him shall see; but those who sit in the shadows of death, are ye who are from among the Gentiles; for ye have been among the shadows of death, ye who have trusted in the worship of idols, and have not known God; but when Jesus the Christ, our Lord and Teacher, was seen by us, a light dawned upon you, in that ye have gazed on and trusted in the promise of an everlasting kingdom, and ye have removed yourselves from the feasts and customs of the former error; and ye worship idols no more as ye worshipped them; but ye have long since believed and have been baptized in Him, and a great light hath dawned upon you. Thus therefore because the Nation did not obey, there was darkness; but the hearing of your ear, you who are from among the Gentiles, became light. Because of this therefore pray and implore for them, and especially in the days of the passover, that by your prayers they may be found worthy of forgiveness, and may be converted to our Lord Jesus the Christ.)

But it is required of you, my brethren (S. + in the days of the passover), Ap. Con. V. xvii.
that ye (S. + investigate and) keep your fast with all care, (S. + but commence, when your brethren of the Nation keep the Passover); because when our Lord and Teacher ate the Passover with us, after that hour He was delivered up by Judas, and immediately we began to be grieved about what we had done to Him; and the number of the moon is as our number in the numbers of the believing Hebrews. In the tenth of the moon, on Monday, came the priests and the elders to the court of Kaipha, the high
priest, and took counsel to kill Him, but they feared, saying, "Not on the Matt. xxvi. 5

feast-day, lest there be an uproar of the people," because every one was
Cf. Matt. xxi. 46 attaching himself to Him and they held Him to be a Prophet, on account of the wonders that He wrought amongst them. But Jesus was in that day in the house of Simeon the leper, and we were together with Him; He also related to us about what was to happen. But Judas
f. 63 b had gone out from among us in secret, on that Monday[1], hoping to deceive
Matt. xxvi. 15 *sic* our Lord; and he went to the house of Kaipha, where the High-priests and elders were assembled, and he said to them, "What will ye give me, and I will deliver my Lord unto you, when I have opportunity?" And they covenanted with him for thirty pieces of silver. And he said to them, "Get ready young men armed because of His disciples" (S. + that if he should go out by night to a desert place, I may come and lead you; then they prepared the young men, and were ready to take Him). But Judas watched when he could find opportunity to betray Him, (S. + because of the crowds of all the people who had come from every city and every village, up to the temple[2] to keep the Passover in Jerusalem). And the priests and elders (S. + considered and) commanded (S. + and decreed) that they should keep the feast with haste, that they might take Him without tumult; for the people of Jerusalem were occupied in the sacrifice and the eating of the Passover, and all the people from without had not yet come, because they deceived them [about] the days, that they might be reproved before God that they were greatly mistaken in everything. So they anticipated and kept the Passover three days earlier, in the eleventh of the moon on Tuesday; for they said, because that all the people go astray after Him, now that we have the opportunity to take Him; and then when all the people have come, we will kill Him before all men for His fault, and this will be known openly, and all the people will turn from after Him. Thus in the night (S. + when Wednesday dawned) Judas delivered up our Lord, but they had given the reward to Judas when he covenanted with them (S. + on the tenth of the moon) on Monday. Therefore it was considered by God, as if they had taken Him from Monday (S. + because that on Monday they consulted how to take Him and to kill
Cf. Ex. xii. 3, 6 Him), and they accomplished their deed on Friday, as it was said in the Book of Exodus, "The Passover shall be kept by you from the tenth to the fourteenth, (S. + on marg., now pay great attention) and then all Israel shall keep the Passover." Therefore from the tenth day, which is Monday, during the days of the Passover, ye shall fast, and be nourished by bread

[1] For a translation of Professor Nau's note on this chronology, see Appendix.

[2] Probably ܠܗܝܟܢܐ is a mistake for ܠܗܝܟܠܐ.

and salt and water (S. + only), at the ninth hour, until Thursday. But on
Friday and on Saturday ye shall fast completely, and eat nothing; but assemble yourselves, and wake and pray the whole of the night, with prayers
and supplications, and with the reading of the Prophets, with the Gospel f. 64 a
and the Psalms, with reverence and fear, and intercession, until the third
hour of the night after the Sabbath, and then ye shall cease your fast, for
it was thus that we also fasted, while our Lord was suffering, in testimony
to the three days, and we watched and prayed and implored about the
perdition of the Nation, because they went astray and did not confess our
Saviour. Thus also pray ye, that the Lord may not remember to them
their guilt unto the end, on account of the perfidy which they showed unto
our Lord, but may give them a place for repentance, and conversion
for the pardon of their iniquity; because he that was a heathen, and a
stranger from the Gentiles, Pilate the judge, had no pleasure in the work
of their wickedness, but took water and washed his hands and said, "I am Matt. xxvii. 24
innocent of the blood of this man"; but the people answered and said,
"His blood be upon us and on our children." Herod commanded that he 25
should be crucified, and our Saviour suffered for us on Friday. Therefore
the fast of Friday (S. + and Saturday) is especially required of you, also
the watch and vigil of Friday[1], the reading of the Scriptures and the
Psalms, and the prayers and supplications for sinners (S. + and the expectation and hope of the resurrection of our Lord Jesus, until the third
hour of the night after the Sabbath. Then bring your offerings, and
thereafter eat and enjoy yourselves, rejoice and be glad, because the Christ
is risen, the earnest of your resurrection). Let that be to you an eternal
law until the end of the world. (S. + for those who do not believe in our
Saviour, He is dead, because their hope in Him is dead, but for you who
believe, our Lord and Saviour is risen, because your hope in Him is immortal, and lives eternally. Fast therefore on Friday, because in it the
Nation killed itself in crucifying our Saviour; and on Sabbath again,
because it is the sleep of our Lord, for it is a day when fasting is especially
required), as the blessed Moses (S. + the prophet of all this) has thus commanded; and it was commanded him by God, who knew what the Nation
was about to do to His Son and His beloved Jesus the Christ; as they
denied Moses and said to him, "Who hath made thee a chief and a Ex. ii. 14
judge over us?" therefore he bound them beforehand in mourning at all
times in separating and appointing to them the Sabbath, because they
deserved to mourn (S. + who denied their life), who laid their hands

[1] S. Saturday.

f. 64 b upon Him who gave them life, and delivered Him over to death. Therefore He appointed to them beforehand the mourning of their perdition. Let us look and see, my brethren, that most men in their mourning imitate the Sabbath; thus also those who keep the Sabbath sit in mourning; for he who is in mourning does not kindle a light, nor do the people [1]of the Jews[1] on account of the commandment of Moses (S. + for thus they were commanded by him. He who is in mourning does not wash himself, nor do the people on the Sabbath. He who is in mourning does not furnish a table, nor do the people on the Sabbath), but they prepare it in the evening and put in order for themselves something to eat, because they have a consciousness of mourning that they were ready to lay hands on the Christ. He who is in mourning does not work nor speak, but sits in sadness; thus also do the people on the Sabbath; (S. + for it was said thus to the people about the mourning of the Sabbath) "Thou shalt not lift thy foot to do any work, nor speak any word from thy mouth." Who is it therefore that testifieth that the Sabbath is a mourning to them? The Scripture testifieth and saith,
Cf. Zech. xii. 12 "Then the people shall lament, tribe by tribe; the tribe of the Levites apart, and their wives apart; the tribe of Judah apart, and their wives apart." As also after the mourning of the Christ even until now, on the ninth of the month of Ab, they read in the Lamentations of Jeremiah, and assemble, and wail and lament. But the ninth is called Θ, for the Θ indicates God; therefore they lament about God, about the Christ who suffered; but nevertheless on account of the Christ our Saviour, and about themselves and their perdition. Why, my brethren, doth a man lament, unless he be in mourning? Wherefore mourn ye also for them, on the Sabbath day of the Passover, until the third hour of the following evening; and thereafter rejoice in His resurrection; be glad and rejoice on their account; cease your fast, and the remainder of
f. 65 a your fast of six days offer to the Lord God. Let those who abound in worldly goods serve those who are poor and in want, and succour them diligently, that the reward of your fast may be received. Whenever the fourteenth day of the Passover may fall, thus observe it; for neither the month nor the day corresponds in time every year, but it varies. Therefore ye, when the people keep the Passover, fast and study to complete your vigil in the midst of their unleavened bread. On Sunday be always glad, for every one who afflicts his soul on

[1] S. on the Sabbath.

Sunday is guilty of sin. Therefore also, except at the Passover, no one is allowed to fast during these three hours of the night which is between Saturday and Sunday, because it belongs to that night of Sunday. But nevertheless in that night only fast those three hours of that night, being assembled together, ye Christians who are in the Lord.

CHAPTER XXII.

Commandment about children that they should be given to learn handicrafts, and that they should not learn bad habits of idleness, and at suitable times wives should be given to them that they fall not into sin, and their fathers be held guilty for their sins.

Teach your sons handicrafts which are suitable and helpful to the fear of God, lest by means of idleness they serve voluptuousness, for not being educated by their parents, they wickedly do works like the heathen. Therefore spare them not, but reprove and discipline and teach them, for by correcting them verily ye will not kill them, but rather ye will give them certain life, as also our Lord teacheth us in Wisdom and saith f. 65 b
thus, "Chasten thy son because there is hope for him, for thou shalt beat Prov. xix. 18
(S. + him) with the rod, and shalt deliver his soul from Sheol." And again Prov. xxiii. 14
He saith, "Every one who spareth his rod hateth his son." But our rod is Prov. xiii. 24
(S. + the Word of God,) our Lord Jesus the Christ, as also Jeremiah saw
the rod of an almond-tree. Every one who spareth to speak a word Jer. i. 11
of reproof to his son hateth his son. (S. + Therefore teach your sons the word of the Lord.) Therefore chasten them with blows, and do not spare on account of their youth, by the word of the fear of God, and do not give them the power of rising against you, and against their parents; and let them do nothing without your advice; that they go not with those of their age to assemble and amuse themselves; because thus they learn vanity, and are laid hold of by harlotry and fall. Should this happen without their parents, they and their parents will be themselves guilty in the judgment before God. If again by your permission they are without correction, and you, their parents, sin, ye shall be held guilty on their account before God. Therefore be zealous that in their time ye take wives for them; and marry them, lest in their youth, in the fire of their adolescence, they commit fornication like the heathen, and ye shall give answer to God in the day of judgment.

CHAPTER XXIII.

About heresies and schisms; that those are condemned to the Gehenna of fire who split the Churches, like Korah and Dathan and Abiram, those who wished to split Israel. Teacheth that the Church of God is one, and that the Churches of heresies are not Churches of God.

Before everything beware of all odious heresies, and flee from them as
f. 66 a from a burning fire, and from those who adhere to them; for if a man in making a schism, condemneth himself to the fire with those who err after him; what shall it be if a man go to steep himself in heresies? for know this, that if any of you love preeminence or venture to make a schism, he will inherit the place of Korah and Dathan and Abiram, he and those who are with him, and also with them he will be condemned in the fire. They also of the house of Korah were Levites, and they served in the Tabernacle of witness. They loved preeminence, and coveted the high-priesthood, and began to speak evil things against that great Moses, as that he had espoused a heathen woman, because he had an Ethiopian wife, and he was defiled by her. Many others of the house of Zambri were with him who committed fornication with Midianitish women, and that the people were defiled along with him. His brother Aaron was the leader in the worship of idols, who made images and sculptures for his people; and they spoke wicked things against Moses, him who did all these signs and wonders from God to the nation, him who had done these glorious and perfect works for their help; him who had brought upon Egypt ten plagues, him who had divided the Red Sea, and raised the waters like a wall on either side, and made the people pass over as in the dry wilderness; and had drowned their enemies (S. + and evildoers and all who were with them); him who had sweetened for them the fountain of waters; and from the flinty stone had brought them out streams, and they had drunk (S. + and been satisfied); him who had brought down to them manna from heaven, and with the manna had given them flesh; him who had given them a pillar of light (S. + for light and guidance) by night, and a cloud for a shade by day; and in the desert had stretched
f. 66 b out a hand to them for the dispensation of the Law, and had given them also the Ten Commandments of God. They spoke evil things against the friend and servant of the Lord, as if to be glorified in righteousness and to boast in holiness and to exhibit purity, and in hypocrisy they showed religion. They also said thus as sober and sedate in holiness,

We will not be soiled with Moses and the people who are with him, for they are polluted. Two hundred and fifty men arose, and led [them] astray in leaving that great Moses, as if they hoped for themselves that they would the better glorify God, and zealously serve Him; for in that multitude of the people it was said, for one censer of perfumes was offered to the Lord God, but those who were in the schism were two hundred and fifty with their leaders; every one of them offered a censer of perfumes to God, two hundred and fifty censers, as those who were more pure and zealous than Moses and Aaron, and than the people [1]of the Lord[1]; but the multitude of the service of their censers which was in schism was of no advantage to them; but a fire was kindled from before the Lord and devoured them; and these two hundred and fifty men were burnt while they were still holding the censers in their hands; and the earth opened her mouth and swallowed Dathan and Korah and Abiram, and their tents and their vessels and all that was with them, and they went down alive to Sheol. The chiefs of their error of schism were swallowed up by the earth (S. + but these two hundred and fifty men who went astray were burnt in the fire, all the people looking on). The Lord spared the rest of the multitude of the people, though there were many sinners amongst them; the Lord judged each one of them according to his works. The Lord spared the multitude of the people; but those who thought that they were purer and more holy and had done more service the f. 67a
fire devoured because they were in schism. And the Lord said unto Moses and unto Aaron, Take the censers of brass from out of the burning, Cf. Numbers xvi. 37
and make them into thin plates, and strew them upon the altar, that the children of Israel may see, and not add to their sins by doing thus, (S. + and pour out the strange fire there, because the censers of the sinners are hallowed in their souls, in the fire; the Lord hath condemned to fire, in that fire came out from before the Lord, and burnt those who put on the incense, which was not permitted to them). Let us look then, beloved, at the latter end of schisms, what happened to them; because if they appear to be pure and holy, their final consummation is in fire and everlasting burning. Let this therefore be a cause of fear to you, for the fire of schism is also judged by fire (S. + not because it sanctified the censers, for they sanctified them through themselves), that is to say, because the fire finished its work, for these people thought in their hearts that their censers were holy; for it was necessary that the fire which was

[1] S. who were with them.

taken for the service of transgression (S. + and for the irritation of God) should not obey them, but should cease from its work or be quenched, and should not consume anything that was put upon it; for now it would not have done the will of the Lord, but would have obeyed schism. Therefore it was said, Pour out there also the strange fire, that is to say, that the Lord judged fire by fire; (S. + if therefore this curse and judgment are appointed for these schisms that think they are praising God,) what will happen to these heresies which blaspheme against Him? but ye from the Scriptures and with the eyes of faith, seeing the plates of brass that are encrusted on the altar, be careful not to make a schism, and not to fall into judgment, but therefore, as believing and intelligent people, keep far away from schisms, (S. + and come not near to them, not even in anything, as Moses said about them to the people,
Numbers xvi. 26 "Separate yourselves from among these cruel people, and come not near to anything that is theirs, that ye perish not with them in all their sins." Whilst the wrath of the Lord was burning about the schism, it is written
Numbers xvi. 34 that the people fled from them, saying "Lest the earth swallow us also with them." Thus ye also, like people who make a struggle for your lives, flee from schisms, and reject those who wish to do thus, for ye know the place of their condemnation. But about heresies, do not even wish to hear their names, and do not defile your ears, for not only do they not verily praise God, but they even verily blaspheme Him, [*marg.* nor does the Lord have pleasure in the prayers of the heretics, nor their supplications, nor their praises.] Therefore the heathen will be judged because they knew
Matt. xviii. 7 not) [1]and offences and divisions, as our Lord said, "Woe to that man by whose means the offence cometh; it were right for him and better for him that a millstone of an ass were hung about his neck and he were drowned in the sea[1]." But the heretics, because they oppose God, are guilty, (S. + as also our Lord and Saviour Jesus said, "There shall be
Matt. xviii. 7 heresies and schisms," and again, "Woe unto the world because of offences! for it must needs be that offences and schisms come, but woe to that man by whose means they come," then we verily heard) but now we verily see,
f. 67 b
Jer. xxiii. 15 as also the Scripture hands down by means of Jeremiah, that "profanity[2] and heresies have gone out into all the land" (S. + as if to persuade our heart) and to confirm our faith that the prophecies are sure; for behold they exist and have been accomplished; because of all the work of the Lord our God, the Lord has turned it from the Nation to the Church by means

[1] S. omits. [2] S. impurity.

of us the Apostles, and He hath removed and forsaken the Nation,
(S. + as it is written in Isaiah, that He hath forsaken the people of the house Is. ii. 6
of Jacob), and Jerusalem is forsaken; and Judah is fallen, and their tongues
are in iniquity, and they have obeyed not the Lord, (S. + and He hath
abandoned the vineyard), and behold, your house is left unto you desolate. Matt. xxiii. 38

CHAPTER XXIV.

That God hath left the Synagogue of the Nation, and hath come to the Church of the Gentiles; and that Satan also hath removed from the people of the Jews, and doth not tempt them any more; and he hath also come against the Church, that he may make in it sects and divisions; and first he raised up in it Simon Magus, afterwards the false Apostles, those from among the Jews who obliged the Christians to act as Jews.

God therefore hath left the Nation, and hath filled the Church, and
hath considered her the mount of [His] habitation, and the throne of
glory, and the house of exaltation; and as David said, "The mountain of God Ps. lxviii. 15
is a mountain of fat, a mountain of arches. What think ye, ye arched 16
mountains; this is the mountain which God hath chosen to dwell in; the
Lord will tabernacle in it for ever." (S. + Ye see therefore how He speaketh
to others, "What think ye?" to those who erroneously suppose that there are
other Churches), for one only is the Church which is the mountain of the
Sanctuary of God. Isaiah also hath said, "There shall be in the latter Is. ii. 2
days (S. + He shall establish) the mountain of the House of the Lord God
of Jacob (S. + in the top of the mountains and higher than the heights),
and all nations shall flow unto it, and many peoples shall go and say, Come, 3
let us go up to the mountain of the Lord; let us learn His way and walk
in it"; (S. + and again he hath said, "There shall be signs and wonders Is. viii. 18.
in the midst of the people from the Lord of Sabaoth, and Him that
dwelleth in Mount Zion," and in Jeremiah also He hath said, "A high throne Jer. xvii. 12
is the house of our Sanctuary"). Because therefore the Lord hath forsaken
the nation of Israel, He hath also abandoned the temple (S. + He hath
made them desolate, and cloven the veil of the door), and taken away from
it the Holy Spirit (S. + and cast it on those who believe from among
the Gentiles, as He hath said by means of Joel, "I will pour out of My Joel ii. 28
Spirit upon all flesh,") and the power of His Word, and He hath taken
away all service from the Nation, and hath established it in the Church f. 68 a
of the Gentiles. In like manner also, Satan the Tempter hath gone away

from that Nation, and hath come upon the Church, and henceforth he will not tempt that Nation, because the Holy Spirit hath left it, for by their wicked works they have fallen into his hands, but he prepares to tempt the Church, and to do his works in her, and to raise against her afflictions and persecutions and heresies and schisms (S. + and before that time there were in that Nation heresies and sects; but now Satan, by his wicked energy, sent out those who belong to the Church, and caused heresies and sects).

About Simon Magus.

The beginning of heresies was thus. Satan possessed a man, Simon, who was a magician, and who had formerly been his servant; and when we, by the gift of the Lord our God and the power of the Holy Ghost, were doing miracles of healing in Jerusalem, and by means of the laying on of hands the gift and fellowship of the Holy Spirit were being given to those who came near, then Simon offered us much silver, and wished that as he had deprived Adam of the knowledge of life by means of the eating of the tree, thus also by the gift of silver he should deprive us of (S. + the gift of) God; and (S. + by the gift of a possession) should get hold of our mind, so that we might exchange and give him for silver the power of the Holy Ghost; and we were all shaken about this. Then Peter looked
Cf. Acts viii. 20, 21 at Satan, him who dwelt in Simon, and said to him, "Thy money go with thee to perdition; and thou shalt not have any part in this word."

About the false Apostles. But when we had divided all the world into twelve parts, and had gone out among the Gentiles to preach the Word, then Satan wrought and excited the Nation; and they sent after us false Apostles to destroy the Word; and they sent out from the Nation one whose name was Cle[o]bius, and he adhered to Simon, but also to Theuda,
f. 68 b and to Judah the Galilean, as well as to others after them. But Simon's people adhered to me, Peter, and came to destroy the Word. When he was in Rome, he greatly troubled the Church, and perverted many, and showed himself as if he were ready [1]to ascend to Heaven[1]; and captivated the Gentiles, exciting them by the power of the energy of his sorceries. One day I went and saw him in the market deceiving the people; we had a dispute with each other about the Resurrection and about the life of the dead; and when he was conquered, he pretended to fly in the air, and began to give a sign to his gang to raise him. And when he had risen to a great distance, then I stood and said to him, "By the power of the name

[1] S. to fly.

of the Christ, I cut off thy powers that they depart from thee." Then the demons departed from him, and he fell, and was broken from the heel of his foot, and he died. And many turned from him; but others, who were worthy of him, remained with him; thus first his heresies were fixed. But also by means of other false Apostles the Enemy wrought. They all had one Law on the earth; and they did not recite either the Torah or the Prophets, and they blasphemed against the Father, God Almighty, nor did they believe in the Resurrection; but also in other things they taught and excited with many opinions; for many of them taught that no man should take a wife, and said that when a man did not take a wife it was Holiness. By means of holiness, and for its name, they praised the weak opinions of their heresies. Again, others of them taught that a man should not eat flesh, and they said that it is not right for a man to eat anything that has f. 69a
life in it. Others said that he must keep himself from swine, and that he may eat the things that the law cleanses (S. + and circumcise as in the Law). Others again taught otherwise, and made strifes, and troubled the Church.

CHAPTER XXV.

Teaches that the Apostles assembled and settled the disputations and confusions that were in the Church, and cured the scandals that the false Apostles had wrought in it; and freed the people of the Christ from the burden of the observances of the law of Moses; and wrote writings to all the Churches of the Gentiles about what it was necessary for them to observe; and they wrote this Didascalia. We therefore have begun to preach the Holy Word of the Catholic Church. We returned again to visit the Churches, and found them of different opinions; some observed as holiness, thinking marriage profane, and some abstained from flesh and from wine, and some from swine's flesh; and they kept all the bonds that are in Deuteronomy. When therefore a danger arose that heresies should be in all the Church, we assembled together, the twelve Apostles, in Jerusalem, and considered about what was to be. It pleased us all with one mind, to write this Catholic Didascalia, for the assurance of you all; and in it we confirmed and appointed that ye should worship God (S. + the Father) Almighty, and His Son Jesus the Christ, and the Holy Ghost, and that ye should minister in the Holy Scriptures, and believe in the Resurrection of the dead, and make use of all His creatures with thankfulness, and take wives, for He said in Proverbs, that "from God the wife is betrothed to the Prov. xix. 14

f. 69 b man," and in the Gospel our Lord said, that "He that created in the
Matt. xix. 4 5 beginning the male hath said that He created also the female[1]. Therefore
shall a man leave his father and his mother, and shall cleave unto
6 his wife, and they twain shall be one flesh; what therefore God hath
joined together let no man put asunder." But the spiritual circumcision
Jer. iv. 3 of the heart is sufficient for believers, as it is said in Jeremiah, "Light
sic 4 a lamp for yourselves; sow not among thorns" (S. + "circumcise to the
Lord your God; circumcise the foreskins of your hearts, ye men of
Joel ii. 13 Judah"; and again in Joel He saith, "Rend your hearts and not your
garments"). About Baptism also, this one alone is sufficient (S. + to you),
the one which has completely taken away your sins; for Isaiah did
Is. i. 16 not say "Be ye washed," but "Wash yourselves once and be clean." But
we had a long disputation, as men who wrestle for the sake of life; it was
not among us the Apostles only, but also among the people, with James
the Bishop and Saint of Jerusalem, him who according to the flesh was
brother of our Lord, (S. + and with his Elders) and the Deacons [2]of the
Cf. Acts xv. 1 Church of Jerusalem[2]. Because also some days before men had come
down from Judæa to Antioch, and had taught the brethren, "Except ye be
circumcised, and conduct yourselves according to the Law of Moses, and
be cleansed from meats (S. + and from all the other things), ye cannot be
saved." And they had much vexation (S. + and disputation). [3]The
brethren of Antioch did not know[3] that we were all assembled and come
in order to examine about these things; they sent to us believing men who
were acquainted with the Scriptures, that they might learn about this question,
(S. + and when they were come to Jerusalem, they told us about the
Acts xv. 5 dispute) which they had in the Church at Antioch. But some men of the
doctrine of the Pharisees who believed arose and said, "Ye ought to be
circumcised, and to keep the Law of Moses," (S. + and others also cried
Cf. Acts xv. 7 ff. out and said thus). Then I Peter rose and said unto them, "Men and our
brethren, ye also know that from the first days when I was among you,
f. 70 a God chose that by means of me the Gentiles should hear the Gospel and
believe; and God, who searcheth the hearts, bare witness to them, to
Cornelius the Centurion, when the Angel appeared to him, and spoke to
Cf. Acts x. 9–16 him about me, and he sent for me. But while I was getting ready to go to
him, it was revealed (S. + to me) about the Gentiles who should believe, and
about all meats; for I went up on a roof to pray; and I saw the Heavens
opened, and a garment bound at its four corners, and it was let down and

[1] This passage stands nearly thus in the Old Syriac.

[2] S. and with all the Church.

[3] S. When the brethren of Antioch knew.

descended to the earth, and in it were all four-footed beasts and creeping
things of the earth and fowls of the heaven; and there came to me a voice
saying, Simon, rise, slay and eat. And I said, Be it far from me, Lord, to
eat anything that is impure, (S. + for I have never eaten anything that is
impure and polluted). And another voice came to me the second time,
saying, What God hath cleansed, call not thou common. But this was done
three times, and it was lifted up from me into heaven. Then I considered
and knew the word of the Lord, that as He said, Be glad[1], ye Gentiles, Deut.
with the people, (S. + and that in every place He hath spoken about the xxxii. 43
calling of the Gentiles). And I rose and went; and when I entered
his house, I began to speak the Word of the Lord; the Holy Ghost Cf. Acts x.
rested upon him and upon all the Gentiles who were present there. 44
God therefore gave them the Holy Spirit, even as unto us, and made no Cf. Acts xv.
difference in faith between them and us, and purified their hearts. Now 8 9 10
therefore why tempt ye God, to put a yoke upon their necks, which neither
our fathers nor we were able to bear? But by the goodness of our Lord 11
Jesus the Christ, we believe that we shall be saved even as they; for the
Lord hath come to us, and hath loosed us from these bonds, and hath said f. 70b
to us, Come unto Me, all ye who are weary and carry heavy burdens, and Matt. xi. 28
I will give you rest. Take My yoke upon you, and learn of Me, for I am 29
quiet and humble in My heart, and ye shall find rest unto your souls, for 30
My yoke is pleasant and My burden is light. If therefore our Lord
loosed us and lightened from us, why do ye wish to put a halter on
yourselves?" Then all the people kept silence, and I James answered and Acts xv. 13
said, "Men and our brethren, hearken unto me. Simon hath declared how 14
God at first did say that He would choose from among the Gentiles a people
for His name; and to this agree the words of the Prophets, as it is written, 15
After this I will raise and build the tabernacle of David which is fallen; 16
and its ruins I will build and raise; that the residue (S. + of men) may 17
seek the Lord, (S. + and all the Gentiles, upon whom My name is called, 18 *sic*
saith the Lord, who knoweth these things from everlasting. Therefore I say, 19
let no man dispute with those who from among the Gentiles are turned to
God), but let us send to them thus: Remove from idols and from sacrifices 20
and from blood and from strangled things." Then it pleased us the Apostles 22
(S. + and the Bishops and the Elders) with all the Church, to choose from
among them men and to send them with those of Barnabas and Paul, who
came from thence; and we chose Judah who was called Barnaba, and Shela,
men distinguished among the brethren, and we wrote these with our hands: 23

[1] Or "Make merry."

Letter of the Apostles. "The Apostles, and Elders and Brethren, to the
Brethren who are of the Gentiles that are in Antioch, and in Syria, and in
24 Cilicia, much greeting. Because we have heard that men whom we have not
25 sent trouble you with words which corrupt your souls; it seemed good to
all of us, being assembled together, to choose and send men to you with
27 our beloved ones those with Barnaba, whom we have sent. But we have
sent Judah and Shela, who also by word will speak to you about these
f. 71 a 28 things: for it hath pleased the Holy Ghost, and us, that no greater burden
29 should be put upon you than that ye remove yourselves from what is
necessary, and from sacrifices, and from blood, and from strangled things
(S. + and from fornication); from these keep yourselves, and ye shall do
good things, and fare ye well in our Lord." But we sent this letter, and
we remained in Jerusalem many days; and we examined and we decreed
together the things that were said[1] to all the people; but further we
wrote also this Catholic Didascalia.

CHAPTER XXVI.

Showeth that from the first the Apostles turned to the Churches of the Gentiles, as from the beginning of preaching, and in passing among them, they fixed and confirmed them, and appointed Canons among them. The
opinion therefore which we have counselled and considered about those
who were formerly in error, and we have sent and decreed, is thus, that we
should return again anew, and also go to the Churches a second time, as
from the beginning of preaching; we should also confirm believers, that
they should avoid the before-named offences, that they receive not those
who come among them falsely in the name of the Apostles, and that they
distinguish them by the difference between their words, and the effects of
Matt. vii. 15 their deeds, because these are those of whom our Lord said that there
shall come to you men wearing sheep's clothing, but inwardly they are
16 ravening wolves; and by their fruits ye shall know them. Beware of
Cf. Matt. xxiv. 11 them therefore, for false Christs and lying prophets shall arise, and shall
12 deceive many, and because of the greatness of iniquity, the love of many
13 shall wax cold; but he that shall endure unto the end, he shall be saved.
Those therefore that have not been deceived and those who repent of
f. 71 b error, they shall be left in the Church; but those who hold fast the error

[1] S. helpful.

and repent not, we cut off and appoint that they go out of the Church, and
be separated from the believers, because they have heresies, (S. + in order
to command the believers, to keep entirely away from them), and they should
have no communion with them either by word or by prayer; for these people
are the enemies (S. + and spoilers) of the Church; for about these our Lord
hath commanded us and said unto us, "Beware of the leaven of the Pharisees Matt. xvi. 6
and of the Sadducees"; and "Into the cities of the Samaritans enter not," Matt. x. 5
(S. + but the cities of the Samaritans are of heresies), which walk in a crooked
way (S. + of which He spake in the Proverbs, "there is a way that men think Prov. xiv. 12
straight"), "and its end leadeth lower than Sheol." These are they against xvi. 25
whom our Lord decreed severely and bitterly, and said, "They shall not be Matt. xii. 32
forgiven, neither in this world, nor in that which is to come," (S. + for
because of the Nation which did not believe in the Christ, and laid hands
upon Him, on the Son of man, that laid hands on Him blaspheming; and
our Lord said, "It shall be forgiven unto them"; and again our Lord said
about them, "My Father, they know not what they do, nor what they Luke xxiii. 34 *sic*
speak; if it be possible, forgive them"; but again also the Gentiles
blaspheme against the Son of man, because of the Cross, and to them he hath
also given forgiveness), to those who believed (S. + of the Nation or) of the
Gentiles by means of baptism, and blasphemed, He hath not given the
pardon of their wicked deeds, as the Lord the Christ hath said, "Wherefore Matt. xii. 31 *sic*
I say unto you, that all sins and blasphemies shall be forgiven unto men;
but the blasphemy against the Holy Ghost shall not be forgiven, neither in
this world nor in that which is to come; and every one who speaketh a 32
word against the Son of man, it shall be forgiven him; for every one that
blasphemeth against the Holy Ghost shall not be forgiven, (S. + neither in
this world, nor in the world to come). Those who blaspheme against the
Holy Ghost, those who against God Almighty hastily and hypocritically
blaspheme, (S. + those heretics who receive His holy Scriptures, or who
receive them wickedly in hypocrisy with blasphemy, or who blaspheme by
wicked words against the Catholic Church, which is the receptacle of the
Holy Ghost, are those who before the future judgment and before the
Spirit, have from of old been condemned to give answer before the
Christ; for this which He said, that "it shall not be forgiven unto them,"
is a sentence of severe punishment of the condemnation which expels
them), and say that the Holy Ghost does not dwell in baptism, nor in
the flesh and blood of the Christ. Having decreed and established
and confirmed with one mind, each one of us went out and departed
to his first portion, confirming the Churches, because the things that had

been predicted were fulfilled, and disguised wolves had come, and false
f. 72 a Christs and lying prophets had appeared; for this was known and manifest that when (S. + the times) should approach (S. + and His coming be near, there should be more and worse than these, from whom may the Lord God therefore deliver you!) may they also repent of their godless error, and by much admonition and by the word of doctrine of prayer we have cured and healed and forgiven in the Church[1]. Those who [2]restrain the word[2] by the perverted word of error, and there is no cure for them, we put out, that they may not [3]lead the holy Church astray[3], the pure Church of God; lest like a hateful leprosy and like a cancerous ulcer it should get to every one; but that pure and unpolluted and passionless and spotless, the Church may be sealed to the Lord God, they who are in every place and in every city, and in all the habitable part of the world. We make and testify; and we leave this *Didascalia*, holy and Catholic, justly and righteously to the Catholic Church, and for the assurance of believers.

[1] S. Churches.
[2] S. are mortally wounded.
[3] S. pollute the Holy Catholic Church.

APPENDIX.

Translation of note by Professor Nau on the Chronology contained in Chapter XXI. (*La Didascalie*, p. 119).

"There are numerous discussions on the chronology of the week of the Passion.... The greatest difficulty consists in conciliating the Synoptics with St John. The *Didascalia* does not think of this conciliation, for it seems to ignore the Gospel of St John, but nevertheless it furnishes a solution. (On Sunday Jesus announces that in two days it will be the Passover, and that the Son of man will be delivered up to be crucified.) On Monday the chief priests assemble, and decide to seize Jesus and to keep the Passover on Tuesday. On this Monday Jesus was in the house of Simon the Leper. As Friday is to count for two days, that really takes place, as St John says, six days before the Passover or the Saturday. For the evening of Friday, when the Passover was usually celebrated, was the commencement of Saturday. Thus the Synoptists and St John speak, the first of the day on which the Passover was celebrated that year, and the second of the day on which it ought to have been celebrated. All are then right; it was enough that we should understand them. Next, our Lord celebrates the Passover on Tuesday; He is arrested on the night following Tuesday, that is to say, on Wednesday; He passes Wednesday in the house of Caiphas, Thursday in the house of Pilate; He is crucified on Friday. At His death darkness covers the earth, which makes two days of Friday, and allows it to be said that our Lord appeared to be dead during three nights, namely, the supplementary night consisting of the darkness which followed His death, the night from Friday to Saturday, and the night from Saturday to Sunday. This explanation, if it had been imagined in our day, would be worthless, but as it has been written at the latest in the third century, it may rest upon a tradition still more ancient, and ought not to be rejected without examination."

CAMBRIDGE: PRINTED BY J. AND C. F. CLAY, AT THE UNIVERSITY PRESS.

For EU product safety concerns, contact us at Calle de José Abascal, 56–1°, 28003 Madrid, Spain or eugpsr@cambridge.org.

www.ingramcontent.com/pod-product-compliance
Ingram Content Group UK Ltd.
Pitfield, Milton Keynes, MK11 3LW, UK
UKHW030902150625
459647UK00021B/2660